I AM ROE

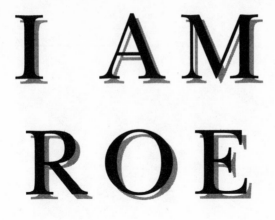

I AM ROE

MY LIFE, *ROE* v. *WADE*, AND FREEDOM OF CHOICE

NORMA McCORVEY

WITH ANDY MEISLER

HarperCollins*Publishers*

HarperCollins books may be purchased for educational, business, or sales promotional use. For information, please write: Special Markets Department, HarperCollins Publishers, Inc., 10 East 53rd Street, New York, NY 10022.

Designed by C. Linda Dingler

Library of Congress Cataloging-in-Publication Data

McCorvey, Norma, 1947–
   I am Roe : my life, *Roe* v. *Wade,* and freedom of choice / Norma McCorvey with Andy Meisler. — 1st ed.
      p.   cm.
   Includes index.
   ISBN 0-06-017010-7
   1. McCorvey, Norma, 1947– . 2. Roe, Jane, 1947– . 3. Women social reformers—United States—Biography. 4. Pro-choice movement—United States—History. I. Meisler, Andy. II. Title.
HQ1413.M34A3   1994
363.4'6'092—dc20   92-56216

94 95 96 97 98 ❖/RRD 10 9 8 7 6 5 4 3 2

For all the Jane Does who died for Choice

Acknowledgments

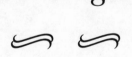

Writing an autobiography of this nature is often a painful and lonely task. The following people helped to ease the burden: Henry Forbes, Jr., Michael Gautreaux, Wavia Gautreaux, Michael Manheim, Alice McLean, Olin J. Nelson, Deanna Pepe, David Steinberg, Marva Williamson, and Celia Ulloa.

Special thanks to Eric and Maureen Lasher, our agents, and Jennifer Hull, our editor.

And much, much love to Connie Gonzales.

Authors' Note

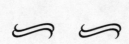

Names marked with an asterisk have been changed to protect the individuals' privacy.

~ 1 ~

My name is Norma McCorvey. But you know me as "Jane Roe." Twenty-one years ago, when I was poor and alone and pregnant, I was the plaintiff in *Roe* v. *Wade*. This was the Supreme Court case that gave American women the right to choose abortion, to control their own bodies, lives, and destinies. To overturn *Roe* v. *Wade*—to make abortion illegal again—is one of the main goals of the Republican party, the Catholic church, and other powerful people who call themselves "pro-life."

In the lawsuit, I was called Jane Roe to preserve my privacy. For many years after that I remained anonymous. Some people think that Jane Roe's real name is still a secret. But in the 1980s, with so much that women had gained being threatened, I decided to break my silence. This was hard for me, because I am basically a shy and private person with a country accent and without much of a formal education. My memories of the *Roe* years are very painful ones. But I feel that I have to speak out.

These days I live in Texas, where I've spent most of my life, in a small house on the outskirts of Dallas. I share it with my best friend of more than twenty years, Connie Gonzalez. We are not rich. Our truck is twelve years old. Sometimes we have trouble paying our bills. I do not have a credit card or a savings account.

I am forty-five years old, the mother of three grown daughters. I work as a cleaning woman, straightening people's apartments and houses and doing their laundry. When I can get time off from my job I travel around the country, speaking at colleges and to women's groups.

People's reactions to me are very different. To some people I am a famous person, a name or a page or a paragraph out of a civics textbook. Once, at a rally in Washington, D.C., Jesse Jackson stood me next to Rosa Parks, the woman who started the civil rights movement in Birmingham, Alabama. This was a little confusing and embarrassing, because it is certainly not how I see myself. How could anyone? Others see me as some kind of heavy-duty feminist theorist, or even a politician. This is so far from the truth of things that it makes me laugh.

On the other hand, many of the "pro-life" people see me as a demon. To them I'm a blasphemer and a baby-killer whose soul they have to "save." Some anti-abortion campaigners have strange ideas about how to do this. Over the years I have had hate mail sent to me, eggs thrown at my house, shotguns fired at my front door and windows, and baby clothes scattered on my front lawn. This frightens me, and on days when I am not feeling especially charitable, it makes me angry.

I take comfort and pride that many women (and men!) have supported and protected me from the pro-lifers. Unfortunately, to some in the women's movement, I am also a nuisance. An embarrassment. An accidental part of their lives, their community, and not to be held up as an example for anybody or anything.

This makes me very sad. All my life I have tried to do my best. The problem, as I try to understand it, is that I do not fit many people's idea of a historical role model. For one thing, I am a women who loves women. For much of my life, I have openly lived a lesbian lifestyle.

For another, I am not a gentle woman. Or a sophisticated one. Unlike many of the women I admire, I have not been able to spend a lifetime thinking of big issues or political strategies or, many times, even what I am going to do the next day or hour or minute.

I would like to be that kind of woman. But I am not. Instead, I am a rough woman, born into pain and anger and raised mostly by myself. I went to reform school, not high school or college. I have had many jobs, but no professions. I have abused drugs and alcohol. I was married to a man who beat me when I was pregnant. I have sought out and pulled close to bad people, and I have lashed out at and pushed away the people who love me. I have a bad temper, and oftentimes, at the worst times, I lose it. I am my own worst enemy. I have had three children—but two of them, for better or for worse, are unknown to me. Of my many sorrows, this is without a doubt the worst.

Others, I know, have suffered just as much as me. Until recently, I worked as a telephone counselor in an abortion clinic. Five days a week, Mondays through Saturdays with Wednesdays off, I took calls from women from as far away as Arkansas, Louisiana, and Mexico. Because of the pressure from "pro-life" activists, there are fewer and fewer places these days for women to get safe, legal abortions.

The clinic I worked for performs abortions up to the twenty-fourth week. It is owned and run by an experienced gynecologist, a kind and generous foreign-born man I admire very much. On Tuesdays, the clinic's patients come in for their examinations. On Thursdays, Fridays, and Saturdays, Doctor performs the procedures. The clinic is spotlessly clean, and everyone is friendly. There are comfortable couches, pretty pictures on the walls. There are brochures and booklets about birth control methods, AIDS prevention, and other women's health problems. There are nurses and social workers available for counseling sessions.

Outside, in front of the clinic, "pro-life" demonstrators walk back and forth. They are present most days, if the weather is good. They are mostly young, conservatively dressed men. They carry pictures showing dead fetuses—photographs blown up hundreds of times—and placards saying that we dismember dead babies and store them in our freezer. Others say that we vacuum live babies out of their mothers' wombs. The right-to-lifers shout and pray at the top of their lungs and try to scare our patients from entering the building. They say that thousands of women have died in legal abortions. They tell our patients that they will die also, and go to hell.

When there were several demonstrators, or when they were particularly noisy and scary, "my" clients—the women I'd made appointments for—would call me from a pay phone at the gas station across the street. Then it was my job to go outside and escort them across the street. The demonstrators knew who I was. I answered them by name. One afternoon, pushing through a particularly big crowd, I noticed a man was holding a brand-new sign. It said: FUTURE AMERICAN SOLDIERS KILLED HERE.

Inside, in the clinic waiting room, sit women of all ages, shapes, and sizes. Most of the time they are calm and . . . not happy, but resigned. Most have a husband or boyfriend or parent with them, holding their hands.

While I worked at this clinic, women called to talk to me all day long. They were well-to-do, they were middle-class, they were dirt poor. They were wives. They were women with lovers. They were single women. They were Latino, Anglo, and immigrants from countries I've barely heard of. They were students, the first in their families to go to college, in danger of losing their part-time jobs and dropping out. They were unemployed women, far from their homes, in Texas to look for work. Some of these women were familiar with the procedure, so I just quoted them the price and gave them an appointment. Many others were in trouble, women whose husbands had left them when they learned that their wives were pregnant.

Some of the women were only vaguely aware of what was going on in their bodies. I tried to explain it to them as well as I could. Other women asked me if our clinic had real doctors. I told them: "Yes, ma'am."

Sometimes they'd ask: "Is it right for me to not have this child, to get an abortion?" And I would tell them what I sincerely believe—that it is a woman's personal and private decision, one that only she can make.

Sometimes the callers were desperate. They were not able to imagine how they could ever escape from their problems, and they talked about ending their lives. I told them I knew what they were talking about. I kept them on the line as long as possible and told them that I, Norma, was their new friend and would try to help them.

In these calls, the women reminded me so much of myself, twenty years ago, alone and terrified, that it was quite often too much for me. When these calls ended I had to hang up, leave my desk, and go into the hallway. Then I let myself cry.

*　　*　　*

Am I a role model? No. For much of my life, it is true, I have lived at the bottom edge of American society. For all those years I have battled oppression—but also my own demons. Many times, when I have been confused or desperate or out of control, the demons have had their way with me. Sometimes I have despaired. Sometimes I have lost hope. But I have always gotten hope back again.

That is because even on my lowest days I always knew this: I am only searching—even in my wildest, meanest, craziest, saddest moments at the very bottom—for what everybody else is also looking for—happiness, security, love.

So there is a reason that I was chosen twenty years ago to represent millions of women in a cause that, back then, I barely even knew I was a part of. For since that time, miraculously, I—we—have won many victories. And the cause of reproductive freedom has become a part of me. Even if those millions of women didn't know I existed, I was fighting right alongside them.

I feel very close to all these women. Over the years we have struggled together. We have demanded the right to control our bodies, our lives, our destinies. We have tried to find our place in the world. We have fought the powers that want to keep women second-class citizens. We have grown. We have learned. And we will continue to fight. And live. And love. This is our story. And mine.

2

This much, through both reading about history and living through it, I know: the practice of abortion, for birth control or even for medical reasons, has been as controversial and emotional an issue as there is in this country.

For the last thirty-five years or so, the fight over abortion has rarely been out of the courtrooms or the streets or the headlines. But abortions have been performed as far back as human beings have been on this planet. And almost as far back, people have discussed and debated and fought about whether the practice is illegal or immoral. Almost all of recorded history includes accounts of the argument still being argued today: whether an unborn baby is alive, a human being on its own, or a part of a woman's body—and whether aborting it before term is simply a decision made by a woman about her body . . . or murder.

These days, most Americans don't believe that abortion has anything to do with murder—except for the murder of helpless women unable to find a legal abortion when they need one. Most citizens don't think that abortion should be used as a routine method of birth control. But they do believe that safe, legal abortions should be available to women who want them.

Strictly speaking, abortion is the expulsion of a fetus from the uterus before it has reached the stage of viability. In other words, before the child has the ability to live and breathe on his or her own. This is what the dictionary says. In real life, an abortion can occur in several ways. It can happen spontaneously—the body can expel a fetus for any number of medical reasons related to the mother or the baby. According to doctors, more than three-quarters of all pregnancies are spontaneously aborted, usually at a very early stage.

Or, an abortion can be induced. That means it is brought on purposely, usually by a pregnant woman deciding that she does not want to give birth. During the first trimester (twelve weeks) of a pregnancy, an abortion can be induced relatively easily and painlessly. During the second trimester or later, it gets harder, more expensive, and more medically complicated.

An abortion can be induced for any number or reasons. These include saving the life of the mother, preventing the birth of a child with serious deformities or defects, or as a last-chance form of birth control. Induced abortions are legal in most countries in the Western world. And in areas where abortions are not allowed—in some Moslem countries, for instance—many thousands of them are performed anyway.

We know now that the ancient Greeks and Romans performed abortions. Famous philosophers like Plato and Aristotle wrote and spoke out in favor of it. The early Jewish prophets and rabbis didn't have much to say about it. In the early Christian world, it seems, some holy men and church authorities spoke out against abortion, though others said that God allowed it. But among women, the practice went on practically uninterrupted.

Then a man named Augustine, who lived around 400 A.D. and was later declared a saint by the Catholic church, decided that the only valid reason for sex was for having babies. He said that abortion was a sin. St. Thomas Aquinas, who lived in the thirteenth century, also said that aborting a fetus was a mortal offense against God—but only if the fetus already had a soul. In his opinion, the soul entered the body of a male child forty days after conception. For female babies, it was eighty days.

This attitude, or something like it, was the accepted wisdom for hundreds of years—although until modern times, the Church paid little attention to abortion, concentrating its energy on punishing other sins. English law, which formed the basis of our Constitution, held that abortion was legal up until the moment a fetus "quickened"—which meant when it moved by itself inside its mother's womb. In England, an abortion after quickening became a crime in 1803.

In America just after Independence was declared, abortion was a normal though somewhat undercover part of society. A few state laws against abortion existed, though they were not enforced very often. There were few real doctors, after all, and even the most advanced medicine wasn't too effective back then.

Most women took care of themselves as best they could. They used herbs and folk medicines to induce abortions, and local midwives performed them. Newspapers and magazines advertised abortion-producing drugs, disguised as patent medicines, to cure make-believe female ailments like "blocked menstruation." Every big city had at least one abortionist, usually female—and although she didn't advertise her services, they were well known to the upper-middle class and rich people who could afford them.

All this began to change to change in the mid-1800s. Not because of opposition from priests or ministers, or because the general public had moral objections, but because the medical profession, just becoming organized, wanted to take the practice of abortion away from the unlicensed people who were performing it.

The American Medical Association, made up of men mostly graduated from the brand-new and elite East Coast medical schools, was formed in 1847. It quickly began setting standards for medical procedures and for using the title "Doctor."

By the time of the Civil War, these physicians were speaking out against "criminal" unlicensed abortions and persuading almost every state legislature to pass laws against them. Abortions were morally wrong, they said, and should only be performed for "therapeutic" reasons. In 1873, Congress passed the Comstock Law, which made it illegal to sell, transport, or mail any device designed to prevent conception or cause an abortion.

By 1900, the system was in place. Abortion was illegal everywhere, although a rich or well-connected or fortunate woman could usually get her doctor to perform one in secret. Or, with the consent of his colleagues at a hospital, he could declare an abortion necessary for her physical or emotional well-being.

The rest of America's women made do with secret and dangerous "back-alley" abortions. These were done by drunken and disgraced doctors and dentists, or even totally untrained men and women. Hoodlums and mobsters controlled this part of the abortion business.

A few brave and idealistic doctors performed non-"therapeutic" abortions in secret. But in most cases, women bore children that they weren't ready—financially or emotionally—to support. In the era before real welfare programs, public health services, or women's rights, this had terrible consequences. Millions of women suffered. Hundreds of thousands died: of infection from botched illegal abortions, in unassisted childbirth, or of pure overwork and exhaustion.

Despite the efforts of people like Margaret Sanger, the mother of birth control in the United States, abortion remained a shameful subject. Margaret Sanger was a nurse and social worker and political activist who worked among the poor women and children of New York City. She spread the word that women could take some control over their own reproductive systems—and their own lives.

The Catholic church, though, alarmed that women were talking among themselves about these things, began to back up its old rules with papal encyclicals, sermons, and excommunications. Priests and ministers preached fire and brimstone against the "sin" of abortion. Sanger and her followers were arrested and condemned. Police forces cracked down on this "crime." In the meantime, thousands of women continued to die. If abortion were discussed at all, it was whispered about in dark corners by self-righteous prudes, greedy criminals, and the desperate poor people who were forced to deal with them. It wasn't really until the middle of the twentieth century—the beginning of my lifetime—that things began to change.

❧ 3 ❧

I am a southern woman, half Cajun and part Indian. My maiden name was Norma Leah Nelson. I was born on September 22, 1947, in Lettesworth, Louisiana. Lettesworth is a very small town, deep in the swamps and pine forests, about sixty miles north of Baton Rouge. It spreads itself just a little north and south of State Highway 1, near a sawmill next to the Atchafalaya River. Across a bridge over the river is a slightly bigger town, with a post office and a roadside restaurant, called Simmesport.

My father's name is Olin Nelson, although everyone always calls him Jimmy. My mother's name was Mary Mildred Gautreaux. She was born in Lettesworth, about twenty years before me. I was fourteen before she told me her first name. And even though I asked a few times, she never would tell me her actual date of birth.

My mother's ancestors, who give me my Cajun and Cherokee blood, came to America from France around two hundred years ago. They were shipwrecked onto the coast of Florida, then walked through the Florida Everglades on their way to settling down in Louisiana. Back in those days, my mother told me, Cajun couples got married by holding hands and jumping over a broomstick. My great-grandmother Shin-ver, who lived near us in Lettesworth, was my link to those days. When she was a young woman, Shin-ver smoked a corncob pipe, made her own soap, and boiled her washing in a big iron kettle in the front yard. She lived to nearly one hundred years of age. I loved her very much, and I spent many afternoons rocking and talking to her on her front porch. Right after she was born, I brought my baby daughter Melissa, her great-great-granddaughter, to see her.

"She will have a good life," she told me.

My great-grandmother died a few months later.

My mother's mother, Bertha, married Emar, who had a twin brother, Amos. My grandparents Emar and Bertha had ten children, my uncles and aunts, most of whom are still alive and living near Lettesworth. The entire family lived in a two-room shack. My mother was Bertha's oldest girl.

On my father's side my grandmother was Alma Nelson, who was already old when I was growing up. Grandma Nelson spent most of her life in Texas, but when I knew her she lived in Baton Rouge. She worked as a fortune-teller. She had also been a prostitute and, by the time I knew her, was a madam who owned a whorehouse in Baton Rouge. I would sometimes visit her there. Her hair was dyed flaming red. She drove a big Lincoln Continental, and she wore a mink stole around her neck, even on the hottest days. She was married and divorced or widowed thirteen times. People said that she was probably the most-married woman in the state of Texas. According to what I was told, when she went up in front of the local judge, Judge Richberg, to marry her thirteenth husband, the judge told her: "Alma, you come in here one more damn time with another man, and I am going to put you in jail." Or at least this is the story that was told to me.

My father has told me that he knew his father, a big strapping man, like a lumberjack. He met Mary Gautreaux when he was an army private, a paratrooper who had fought in Europe and was now, at the end of World War II, stationed near Lettesworth. He had been trained to fix radios and radars and other early electronic machinery. When he married my mother he decided to settle down in my mother's hometown. My older brother, Jimmy, was born eighteen months before me.

One day, when I was very young, I overheard my mother saying that when she was pregnant with me, she didn't suspect a thing until her third or fourth month. So she went to the old woman who lived on a country lane nearby and who did all the abortions around Lettesworth. My mother said to her: "Oh, Miz Mary Lee, I've come for you to take my baby." But Miz Mary Lee refused:

"Girl, you can't have no abortion now. It's too late. It would kill you." So my mother was left with no other choice but to have me.

Lettesworth is a typical Cajun town, not really much changed in all the years since I left. The little parish church still has a graveyard, where the dead parishioners lie aboveground in crypts. The men and women work hard during the day, for the state or at the mill or in bigger towns up and down the road, and they get drunk and loud and angry in the local roadhouses at night. Some of my adult cousins have never in their lives been outside the state of Louisiana. Many of the poorer people, mostly black but also white, still live in rundown shacks as old and sad-looking as any in the whole country.

As I remember it, we lived like most people in Lettesworth did. Wet laundry flapped in the breeze all over town. The roads were mostly dirt, unpaved. There seemed to be more junked, rusting cars and trucks than working ones parked on the streets and dumped in the front yards. Our little wood frame house didn't have indoor plumbing, just an outdoor privy, and if a person was smart, he or she would scatter some slop for the hogs—a lot of people raised them and the hogs wandered around the neighborhood without much interference—before using it.

People in Lettesworth, then as now, spoke French and English just about equally. It didn't really make a difference which you used. What did make a difference, though, was keeping in touch with the other world around Simmesport—the one just beyond the regular senses. It was the world of spirits and visions and restless souls that everyone anyone knew believed in totally. The world that was mostly unseen but was as real in its own way as a picture on the wall or a bag of groceries or the lines in the palm of a person's hand. It was this other world that could give clues to the present and future. It could be gotten closer to through dreams, incantations, even voodoo curses, and it could be glimpsed—or even, terrifyingly, reached—with the knowledge passed down from grandmother to mother to daughter.

Because this was certain: the knowledge was women's knowledge, and it could be used only by us. It was not to be shared with outsiders. The consequences of breaking this rule were too terrible to consider. The knowledge was too secret, too dangerous. Too powerful.

* * *

I suppose that in a way I was living in an entirely different country than other children my age—the ones who were riding school buses and watching television shows and wearing Davy Crockett hats.

But I had no idea they existed. The big trucks and fancy cars on the highway never stopped. My mother's sisters, aunts Esther and Jeannie and Sandra, were always having babies and always bringing over new little boy and girl cousins for me to see. During the days the women would do what was called "running the road." That just meant they would go up and down the streets full of houses, visiting. All of them spent most of their free time dropping in on friends and relatives, talking and gossiping and drinking tiny cups of strong French coffee, stronger and more delicious than any I've tasted since.

I had my first cup of coffee at age seven. I had my first beer not long after that. My father liked his beer, and he would get drunk with his men friends most Friday evenings, even though it was during his time in Louisiana that he became a Jehovah's Witness, and according to the rules, Jehovah's Witnesses weren't allowed to drink alcohol or smoke cigarettes. Which he did also.

He didn't seem to worry about it. Maybe I was the only one who did. My father was a short man, but thin and handsome, with coal black hair. Everybody said I looked just like him. During the week he fixed radios and sometimes even television sets. On Sundays he gave speeches in the local Kingdom Hall up the road in Marksville, usually talking about the wages of sin and so forth. We all sat there, in our best clothes, listening to him talk about God and love and redemption.

Later, on weekends, after we moved from the country to the city, we would all get on the bus and ride to different areas of town, knocking on strangers' doors and trying to sell them copies of the Jehovah's Witness magazine, *The Watchtower*. Most people would turn us away, more or less politely. The ones who invited us inside to listen to my father proselytize for hours, usually seemed more than a little strange.

So were we, I suppose. Being a Jehovah's Witness also meant that you weren't allowed to salute the American flag, in school or anywhere else. For this reason, we were always getting called to the principal's office to explain our willful or evil behavior. We also weren't allowed to give or receive Christmas presents or celebrate non-Christian holidays. I am not now a Jehovah's Witness. Maybe I wasn't one back then, either. I just didn't understand their rules at all.

My mother was beautiful. That I realized right from the beginning. She was slim. She had auburn hair, light green eyes, and a perfect figure. She was sexy, sophisticated. A different kind of woman than all the other mothers in Lettesworth.

When we lived in Louisiana she worked as a waitress at Baldwin's Restaurant in Baton Rouge. She looked just about perfect in her waitress uniform—a little checked hat, a tight dress, a bright white apron. She looked just like the Hollywood movie star Rita Hayworth, everybody said. Whether Rita Hayworth was as strong as my mother, or as strong-willed, or as angry at her own daughter—if movie stars even had daughters—I didn't know.

One of the first memories I have of my mother is of her walking down the street, pulling her sandal off her foot, and smacking a neighbor women on the head, over and over. This was because the day before, this woman's son had hit my brother Jimmy, and he had run off crying. I had gone over there and defended Jimmy by punching her little boy until he ran away.

The next morning this woman had come over to complain. I was glad, at first, to see my mother hitting her, but after a few seconds I felt bad. For the truth was that my mother hit me a lot, also. We never got along. I sassed her and disobeyed her and never managed to make her proud of me. I stayed out too late and came home too soon. I got dirty playing and spilled food at the table and was disgusting.

She called me stupid, and an idiot, and when she was angry, which was just about every time she saw me, she smacked me so hard my head hurt. I never could figure out why she disliked me so. Sometimes I felt she blamed me for Jimmy being slow. Or simply for being a girl.

"You're a stupid goddamn little idiot! You never learn anything! You aren't even as smart as your brother!" she would yell. All I could understand about that was that the words were hurting me.

Sometimes she would lock me up in a closet in the dark for

hours, so I could figure out what I had done wrong. My answers were never the right ones. Then she would get so mad that sometimes she would leave the house and not return to let me out for hours.

In the mornings, before she left for work, she left my brother and me with Miz Rose, a black lady who took care of other people's children in her little shack on the outskirts of town. Miz Rose was a nice lady, and I loved her. All the other kids she took care of were black—all except a beautiful little blond girl, with long straight hair and blue eyes, whose mother picked her up at lunchtime. Being different colors, we were all very shy and standoffish with each other. And though my brother Jimmy was bigger and older, he wasn't very good at learning things, so I had to walk him to school and teach him how to ride a bike and throw a ball and play baseball. That kept us apart from the other kids even more.

After we entered grade school, I made a few friends and felt I fit in better. But never at home. Never with my mother. Sometimes I wondered if there had been a mixup at the hospital, that I wasn't her little girl after all. I was so unlike her. So ugly.

I was a tomboy, and I dressed like a boy and played boy's games. But when I was nine, I began growing up very fast. My mother bought me my first bra, handed it to me, and told me to put it on. I put it on backwards, clasp in front. It was uncomfortable.

My mother sat there and watched me for a moment. Then she laughed. "Come on over here," she said. "Come here and let me show you how to do this."

I was ashamed of my body, and of how ignorant I was. A couple of months later, in the middle of a softball game, I hit the ball hard into the outfield, began to run, and slid hard into second base. When I got up I realized that my pants were full of blood.

I had gotten my first menstrual period, but nobody had ever told me about such a thing. I didn't know what was happening. I ran away from the softball field as fast as I could. I thought: I have done something very wrong. God has struck me down. He has put a voodoo curse on me.

We moved to Houston, Texas, soon after that, to a house on Shoreham Drive, on the northeast edge of town. Our neighborhood, completely flat, was filled with paved streets and houses, but it was also filled with trees and dirt roads and vacant lots. It was as if we hadn't yet decided whether we belonged in the city or if we were still country people.

My father went into a business partnership with Jimmy Eddington, a fellow Jehovah's Witness, who everyone knew was the richest man on our street. The reason everyone knew that was because the Eddingtons were the only ones who lived in a house made of brick. Ours was made of wood and raised off the ground on concrete blocks, like everybody else's.

My father and Jimmy's TV repair shop was in the Eddingtons' backyard. My father worked there all day, oftentimes late into the night. Sometimes, to keep myself from talking back to my mother, I'd go over there and watch my father work.

My father would talk about taking my brother and me fishing, which I was always looking forward to, but somehow those fishing trips never happened. Something always came up to stop us. For one thing, my brother wasn't that interested in fishing. For another, there were always people who needed to get their TV sets fixed right away. It wouldn't do at all, he said, to keep them waiting. Eventually, he stopped talking about our fishing trips altogether.

I was lonely, and I missed my old playmates from Louisiana. After a few weeks in Houston, Jimmy Eddington's daughter Nicki introduced me to Marvalynn Williamson, who immediately became my best friend in the world. Marvalynn Williamson was tough. Marvalynn Williamson was cool. She was pretty, she was smart, and she showed me how to smoke cigarettes. To top it all off, she had a great-looking older brother, Larry, who could play piano in any style—jazz, classical, country, or rock and roll. But best of all, he could play and sing just like Jerry Lee Lewis.

Marvalynn Williamson wasn't afraid to talk back to anybody. She'd fight anyone, girl or boy, who made the bad mistake of sassing us or even just getting in our way. And so would I. We were tough girls, Marvalynn and I, and proud of it. I had frizzy hair, impossible to comb. Marvalynn's dark hair was long and beautiful. We roamed the neighborhood, from the Granada Theater to Prince's Drive-In, which was in back of our house. In the afternoons, after school let out, Marvalynn waited for me while I peaked over the Prince's Drive-In fence, checking to see if my mother was home.

If she was, I'd go over to my friend's house for dinner. I was always welcome to eat or sleep there. Marvalynn and I were like sisters. We did everything together, including ditching school, stealing things from the dime store, and hanging out after dinner at the local bowling alley.

After awhile, the men who bowled and drank at the alley got to know us. They liked to give us a few sips of their beer and laugh when we got a little drunk. When they got tired of us, we'd walk home together hand in hand, giggling. If I was lucky my mother wouldn't be fighting with my father. They fought almost all the time now. If I was luckier still, my mother wouldn't be home at all.

One day I came home from school, alone, and felt something was wrong, very wrong. The night before, my parents had had a huge argument, one of their worst. And now something was completely different—I couldn't smell the smoke from my father's cigarettes at all.

"Where's Daddy?" I asked Jimmy.

"He's not here," he said.

That night I slept over at Marvalynn's house. When I came back home the next afternoon my father still wasn't home. I got into a fight with my mother, went into my room and cried, and then I went to bed.

My mother never mentioned the fact that my father had left us, and neither did I. But a few days after that she went to work at Danberg's, a department store, selling sheets and pillowcases. Nights, she worked part-time as a waitress in a Houston nightclub. She'd get home after midnight, hours and hours after Jimmy and I had gone to bed.

She'd go out to the club, too, on nights when she wasn't working. Sometimes when she came home she'd race our car up our street, stopping with a scary squeal of her brakes, and park across the street at a weird angle different from all the other cars. I'd be awake, waiting for her, but I didn't let on.

My mother would come upstairs to my room and sit on my bed, talking to me. Her breath smelled funny, and sweet. It was liquor. I knew that. She'd turn on the light and shake me so I had to open my eyes and look at her.

"Did Jimmy have his dinner?" she'd ask.

"Yes."

"Did Jimmy get his clothes ready for tomorrow?"

"Yes."

"Does Jimmy have his lunch ready for tomorrow?"

"Yes."

"All right, then. Go to sleep."

Then she'd push herself up from my bed and walk away, moving extra carefully, frowning but with her head held high, and go into her own room.

After that I'd stay awake for a long time, thinking.

I'd think about my father. Where was he? Had he really left my mother? Had he forgotten about my brother and me? Would he ever come back? Was he dead?

Or was he off somewhere, divorcing my mother?

I'd think it through. No, he couldn't be dead. Because my father had cause to divorce my mother. She had boyfriends, everybody knew that. Or, at least, she had lots of men friends, men who came around to the house even before my father disappeared. They usually showed up to visit while my father was working. Now, with my father gone, they stayed longer.

Some of them were nice to me. One, I remember, was named Dutch. He drove a bus for Greyhound, and he liked to call me his little girl. I liked that, even though it made me feel a little sad. The truth is, though, that most of my mother's visitors ignored me completely. I decided that was fine with me, too.

About a year later, I came home from school to see our old station wagon parked in the driveway. My father was in the house, smoking a cigarette.

"Oh, we're moving to Dallas," my mother told me.

"Where's that?"

"In Texas."

The same state, I realized. But it was a big state, so we might be going far. We were packed and on the road that same day. I had just enough time to tell Marvalynn good-bye.

In Dallas we lived on McKinney Avenue, in the northeast part of the city. Nowadays McKinney is a fashionable street, filled with shops and restaurants and clothing stores. But back then it was where the poor white working people lived. You could see the big buildings of downtown Dallas from where we were, but it didn't really matter, because nobody we knew ever went downtown. Everything we needed was right there, right where we lived. At the corner of McKinney and Hall was our house. It was old, and made of wood like our Houston house, and we lived on the top floor above another family, the Joneses. My parents had one bedroom. My brother slept in another. I slept in an efficiency apartment on the other side of the building, I had to go out the front door, outside, and walk completely around the porch to get from one apartment to the other.

Across the street, in a house that actually had fireplaces, lived my best friend. Her name was Norma Jane and we'd talk, across the tops of the trees planted in the sidewalks, from our upstairs front porches. Most mornings Norma Jane and I walked together to grade school, which was a just few blocks away. The school was built out of brick and was brand-new.

Pete's, the Italian restaurant where my mother worked, was just a few doors down from our house. Lilly's Lounge, where she spent most of her nights, was right next door. So was Don's Texaco, where I sometimes worked, and eventually robbed.

At the other end of the street was my father's shop. He ran it all by himself, no partners this time, and spent most of his time there. His shop had a sign on the front window that said TV REPAIR, and there was a clock ringed with neon in the window.

My father had barely enough space to work. The shop was filled to the ceiling with strange-looking tubes and wires and circuit boards, and television sets with their insides hanging out. When he took the televisions apart, he'd very carefully put all the tubes into egg crates. Then they had to be tested on the tube-testing machine at the U-Tote 'Em store. He let me take them over and test them for him when I was helping out.

I loved my father very much. He hardly ever raised his voice or criticized me. At that point in his life he was a very quiet man. And a sad man, I think.

And back then I was sad for him, because he worked very hard, and because my mother cheated on him and didn't love him half as much as I did. Some evenings he would grab a beer and a sandwich and take Jimmy and me out to the garage behind the house, which was where he kept his telescope. He would let us look through it, pointing out the stars and planets.

"Norma. Did you finish your. . . ?"

"Yes, Daddy."

"Did you get Jimmy his. . . ?"

"Yes, Daddy."

"Well, okay, then. I'm gonna send you to the moon."

And then he'd show us the moon, and Venus and Mars and Saturn and Neptune, and he pointed out the stars and how they got their names. To me, looking though that telescope, it was like whole new worlds had come into view. They were just too far away, and too pretty to touch.

On Friday nights, Norma Jean and I walked to The Rubiyat, a little restaurant nearby that had just opened. The people inside were too cool! They wore black, both the men and the women, and they were skinny and pale and good-looking. They would close their eyes and snap their fingers to the music playing on the phonograph, which was no music like any we had ever heard. Black men would be sitting at the same tables with white women!

Everybody at The Rubiyat drank wine and smoked cigarette after cigarette. They were beatniks, we knew. Every now and then, one of them would get up and recite poems—which didn't rhyme or tell a story like the ones they made us learn in school. Neither Norma Jane nor I ever worked up the courage to go inside, but we'd stand at the front door and watch. We told each other that we would be beatniks, too, when we grew up.

Beatniks, I told Norma Jane, led wonderful lives. They did what they wanted, when they wanted to do it. They didn't go to school. If they had mothers they didn't like, they just took off and left.

I wasn't yet a beatnik, so I was stuck with my mother. And, as she told me over and over, she was stuck with me. When I needed to talk to her, to tell her that I needed something for school or for Jimmy's dinner, I'd phone Lilly's Lounge, a dark place with dirty floors and a sign that flashed "Open" even when it wasn't.

Sometimes I'd look in to see my mother there, all beautiful and sexy, with men standing around her bar stool. They laughed at her jokes and lit her cigarettes. She'd laugh back at them. And when she wasn't laughing she was smiling, with a face I never saw when we were home.

Sometimes I could reach her at Lilly's. Sometimes I couldn't. "Is my mom over there?" I'd ask the owner of the bar.

Aunt Lilly—she'd asked me call her that—was a nice woman, around fifty years of age, who wore red lipstick and lots of white makeup and sometimes let me go behind the bar and wash glasses for her.

"Well, yeah, honey. She's here. But she can't come to the phone right now," Lilly would say, in the funny voice she used when she was lying. I imagined what was really happening. I imagined my mother getting up from the bar and riding home with a stranger. I was mad and sad at the same time.

One night I asked, "Who'd she leave with, Aunt Lilly?"

Aunt Lilly didn't say anything for a long time. I listened to the bar sounds of glasses clinking and people laughing and shouting from her end of the line. "Well, you know, Norma," she said, finally, "just because she's gone now, it doesn't mean that she's not coming back."

It was around that time, around the school year I turned ten, that the anger inside me started building up to a dangerous level. I was always mad at everyone, and even though I knew what the dangers were I couldn't hold my tongue. When I talked back to her, my mother would slap me. My father was gone even more than usual. In his place were other men, more of them. Jimmy, who was a sweeter boy than ever, with problems that his teachers and doctors were beginning to understand, just looked scared. It got so bad in the house that when school was finished, it wasn't only that I didn't want to go home. Now I was afraid to.

I slept at classmates' houses if I could. If not, I kept myself outdoors as much as possible. At night I sat alone in a nearby park or in the little local cemetery until everyone had gone to bed and I could sneak in through the back door. Then I'd sleep a few hours, wake up—usually from a bad dream—and go out on the porch and think.

In the afternoons and on weekends I'd work at Don's Texaco station, helping out with the gas pumps and checking the oil and tires and washing windshields. Don, the owner, trusted me, and he would go out on service calls or to the barber shop and leave me to run the station all by himself.

I was a short little girl with slicked-back hair, usually wearing jeans and a white T-shirt. The customers paid me, and I made change and left the money in Don's desk. I even locked up the pumps at closing time. I was happy doing this job, and I was proud of myself. But when nightfall came the service station closed down.

After dark I'd walk the streets, making circles around the neighborhood. I was an angry little girl, just walking. One night I was so angry, and walking so fast, that a cruising police car slowed down alongside me.

The cop on the passenger side leaned out his window and yelled, "Hey, kid! Stop! What are you doing here?"

"None of your business. I'm not doing anything wrong. Just leave me alone."

They pulled me inside their police car and told me that if I didn't watch my mouth I'd be in big trouble, that I should think more carefully before I answered their questions.

"Is this how you guys get your grins?" I asked.

Then one of them grinned, and one of them frowned, and he said they were going to arrest me. They drove me downtown to their police station and took me inside and stood me in front of a fat old sergeant. He sat staring at me from behind his big desk.

"Well hell, fellas," said the sergeant. "I thought you said you were bringing a little boy down here. This looks to me like a little girl. Honey, are you a little girl or a little boy?"

I was so angry and scared that I couldn't say anything. Nothing at all. So they called my father to pick me up, and in a few hours he came to take me home. He didn't have to say anything. He just looked sad. He knew my mother would hit me until I screamed and cried. And she did.

To my ten-year-old mind there was only one solution. I had to run away. Far away, where my mother couldn't find me, and where I could start my life all over again. I'd go to Oklahoma City, I decided. I'd seen it on television, on a news program, and I couldn't imagine anybody there would know who I was or care enough to notice me.

In the new life I was planning, I would need friends. So I convinced Christina,* a classmate who'd told me that her home life was awful also, to run away with me. Our first problem, I knew, was money. We didn't have any, and we needed some to travel. No grownup would give us any, and the only place I knew where I could get some was Don's money drawer. I felt bad. I knew it was wrong to steal money from a friend. But I would never come back, so Don would never figure out who had robbed him.

One afternoon while Don was gone I took all the money out of the cash drawer, then called Christina. We walked to the Greyhound bus station and bought two tickets.

The bus pulled out of Dallas. Christina was happy to be escaping, and so was I. As we rolled along she giggled and looked out the window at the countryside. But after awhile, I was worried. I knew we'd need a place to stay in Oklahoma City. I figured they didn't rent hotel rooms to little girls. I needed a plan.

A few hours into the trip, I came up with one. I overheard a lady sitting across the aisle say, "The first thing I'm going to do when the bus stops, is go to Western Union to send a telegram."

That was it. When we finally got to Oklahoma City, we got out and looked around for a hotel. I saw a big building with a sign on it that said: BLACK'S HOTEL.

I stopped an older woman on the street. "Where's the Western Union office?" I asked, and she pointed around the corner.

Just like she said, the Western Union office was right there. "I want to send a telegram to Black's Hotel," I told the man behind the counter. He looked at me a little suspiciously, so I said: "Is there a hotel like that around here?"

"Yes, there is," he said.

"Then I'd like to send a telegram there," I said. "It should go to Miss Norma Leah Nelson. It should say, 'Honey, I'll catch up with you later this evening. Love, Dad.'"

The Western Union man looked confused. "Don't you mean 'Love,' uh, your name?"

"No. It's a kind of secret code my dad and I have for each other."

He looked even more suspicious, but when I paid for the telegram he said he'd send it. I paid him, and then we walked around Oklahoma City seeing the sights for a couple of hours. I told Christina to wait for me back at the bus station.

Telling myself not be scared, I walked by myself into Black's

Hotel. I went up to the front desk, told the clerk my name, and asked if there were any messages for me.

"Oh yes, Miss Nelson. We just got a telegram for you."

I ripped open the envelope and pretended to read it. "Oh, good. My father's coming. He made a reservation for us, right?" No, they said, it turned out that my father had forgotten to call ahead and do that.

"Well, could you rent my father and me a room, anyway?" I pulled out a bunch of Don's money to show them I had some.

The hotel clerk looked a little surprised, but the money was enough so they rented me the room. After the bellhop took me upstairs, I went right back downstairs, ran to the bus station, and told Christina to wait a few minutes, then sneak into Black's Hotel and meet me in our room. It worked.

For almost the next two days Christina and I lived our brand-new lives. We walked around Oklahoma City some more, having a fine old time. We shopped for clothes—shorts, crop tops, fun hats, sunglasses—and ordered room service whenever we felt like it. They brought the hamburgers and french fries right upstairs on a little cart. Then they cleaned up the whole mess the next morning. It was wonderful.

We were very happy. We weren't lonely, and we didn't miss our parents. We weren't even thinking about our parents—that's what we told each other.

I liked living with Christina. We became good friends—best friends, she told me, and I agreed.

On the second morning, while we were sitting on our beds watching television, she told me a secret about this boy we both knew. He had done something to her one night. Had a boy ever done anything like that to me?

"What is that?" I asked Christina.

"This," she said.

Christina started hugging and kissing me, and when she told me I could, I kissed her back.

"Now you're supposed to touch me and kiss me here," she said, showing me where.

I did. It felt good, kissing my best friend. I wanted to get closer to her, somehow, though I didn't know exactly how. I felt feelings moving inside of me, feelings I'd never really felt before.

*   *   *

Then suddenly, as we were kissing and hugging, our door opened. A maid looked in. She took a good long look at us.

"Oh! Excuse me!" she said, with a funny expression on her face.

"That's okay," I said to her, but she had already slammed the door. I knew we were in trouble.

A couple of hours later, the manager knocked on the door.

"What are you two girls doing in there?" he said in an angry voice. "Your father hasn't shown up. Open the door and come outside right this minute!"

We kept the door closed. Thirty minutes later a man who said he was a policeman started to bang on the door.

"Open up, ladies!" he yelled.

"Run, Chris!" I said.

I went through the window and down the fire escape. When I reached the street I ran and ran and ran, to the left and to the right, but after awhile a police car pulled up next to me and, too tired, I stopped. They took me down to Oklahoma City Juvenile Hall.

The policemen put me in a room by myself. Then a big man with a bald head in a white shirt and a skinny tie came in.

"Hi, Norma," he said. He told me that he was a detective.

I knew that. I'd also seen "Manhunt" on television, so I knew what to do. I didn't say anything.

"You know, Norma, your mama's been really worried about you. She had your picture in the newspapers and on television and all."

"You're lying, mister," I told him.

"Well, Norma, I'm not. And I'm telling you this also—you're in a lot of trouble."

He stopped and scowled at me. I could feel my courage draining away.

"Did you rob that filling station?"

I said nothing.

"When you took that money, did you have a knife or a gun? You know, a weapon?"

I kept quiet, my arms crossed and my mouth closed.

"Well, you are not doing too good here, Norma. Things are getting worse and worse for you. So I'm just going to ask one more question, and see if you can make things easier for yourself. Your friend Christina says that you sodomized her. Did you?"

I was safe here, I thought. I didn't know what he was talking about, but I figured that if I'd done to Christina what he'd said I had, I'd have known it.

"I did not!" I said.

"Norma, she said you had your hand in her underpants."

"Yeah, I did that," I said, puzzled. Why did he even care? But he didn't tell me. He just wrote something down in his notebook, smiled a funny little smile, and left me alone in my room.

They put handcuffs on me and drove me back to Dallas in the backseat of a police car. It was just me, with two policemen up front.

The next time I saw my friend Christina—which was also the last time I saw her—was at my family court trial. Christina testified that I'd told her about robbing the filling station, and that I had kissed her all over even though she'd told me to stop.

At the end of my trial I stood up in the courtroom between my mother and father.

The judge, an old man with white hair, said he'd made up his mind, that I'd done most of the bad things they'd said I did, that I had made a very bad start in life, that he would help me change my life around if I wanted to, and that I was now a ward of the state of Texas.

"Norma, I've got half a mind to send you to the State School for Girls in Gainesville," he said.

Then that judge did something I'll never forget. He looked over to my mother for her reaction to my sentence. Say something, Mama, I thought. Tell him not to put me in jail.

I looked closely, and so did the judge, but her expression never changed. She didn't move a muscle.

The judge thought for a second and said he'd changed his mind. He would send me instead to a place called Mount St. Michael's, which was in Oak Cliff, on the other side of Dallas. That's where I would live for the next year. And then he would see if I had decided to become a moral and honest citizen.

* * *

Mount St. Michael's was a Catholic boarding school run by an order of nuns who lived with us. The school was in a big reddish-brown brick building, and I stayed there seven days a week, sleeping with the rest of the girls in a big open dormitory on the second floor. The state paid my tuition. My mother and father, coming separately, each visited me a couple of times.

We wore uniforms: blue skirts and white blouses, blue benie hats, saddle shoes, and bobby socks. In the mornings we went to class on the first floor. In the afternoons we spent three or four hours doing laundry.

The laundry was in the basement. Mount St. Michael's students did all their own laundry, plus all the nuns' laundry, plus laundry that the school brought in from the outside to make money. It was important that the laundry be washed and ironed just right, said the nuns. The school's reputation, and ours, depended on it.

The trouble was, my reputation was dirt. I didn't fit in at all at Mount St. Michael's, and I and everybody else knew it. For one thing, girls came and went so fast that when I made friends with them, my heart was broken when they left. For another, I wasn't a Catholic—or anything else—and I didn't want to become one, even though every nun there tried to convince me that I would go to hell if I refused.

I didn't believe them. I thought I knew more about hell than any of the nuns did, so their preaching made me more determined to fight them. I was one of the few girls there who didn't take catechism class. For such willfulness and disobedience, they said, and because I was putting my mortal soul in danger, I was given extra inspections, tests, homework, and detention. Once I was locked in a music room by myself for two days. They brought in my food and when I was finished they took out my plates and glasses and the chamber pot.

When I got out of detention, I decided to keep to myself as much as possible. I had a secret best friend: John F. Kennedy, our new president. Or maybe he wasn't just my friend. Maybe he was my secret father and boyfriend, all rolled into one.

He was so handsome and smart and powerful that I dreamed of growing up and marrying him. Or, if that wasn't possible, of becoming his daughter and moving into the White House with Mrs. Kennedy and John-John and Caroline. I watched him on TV as much as I could. I read the newspaper articles about him, and I cut them out and kept them in a scrapbook.

One morning, when nobody else was around, a young novice nun came up to me when I was coming out of the shower. She asked me if she could dry off my back. I said okay, and then in the next second she hugged me, kissed me, and pushed me under a dormitory bed. Then she had with me what, I realize now, was sex.

I knew this was wrong, but I never mentioned it to anybody. It must have been my fault, I thought. Because who would have believed me if I had told them otherwise?

That was the only time the novice nun did that to me. A few weeks later they marched us all down to the school chapel, and we watched her take her final vows.

A month or two after that, while I was working in the laundry, Sister All Saints, one of the head nuns, looked at the sleeve of a men's shirt that I had ironed and folded, told me it was wrong, all wrong, and shook it out and told me to do all over again.

I lost my temper. I told her to shove her fucking shirt up her fucking ass, and I cursed and swore at her until the other nuns dragged me away.

After I got out of the music room Sister All Saints called me to her office. She told me I was evil and a bad influence on the other girls, and that she was returning me to the court.

After another hearing, I was sent to reform school after all. They took me to Gainesville, Texas, about two and half hours north of Dallas. It was only a few miles from the Oklahoma state border.

4

In 1914, Margaret Sanger wrote in a newspaper she published: "A woman's body belongs to herself alone."

Later, for promoting birth control, this great woman reformer was arrested under anti-obscenity laws. Government agencies and powerful people all over the country tried to silence her voice.

Her message had gotten out, though. Margaret Sanger founded the American Birth Control League, the forerunner of today's Planned Parenthood. Despite their illegality, birth control methods became widely available—to all those wealthy and educated enough to have access to them and understand their use. This disturbed the Catholic church so much that in 1930, the pope issued an encyclical—a major papal decree—banning "artificial" methods of birth control and abortion forever.

Only the most devout Catholics obeyed, though, because birth control devices had become a part of many couples' lives. Abortions became easier to get in countries like Russia, China, Iceland, and Denmark. Though abortion in America was still a semi-obscene subject, thousands of dangerous, illegal abortions were performed. And although it wasn't discussed much in public, a few thousand legal abortions were performed in hospitals each year. In order to get one of these, a woman almost always had to convince a panel of doctors (usually men) that her health would be in danger if she went through with her pregnancy. Whether this meant physical health or mental health was never really decided—

the standards under which legal abortions were allowed were different in every state and city and hospital.

This humiliating process went on largely behind closed doors. Then, in 1962, the troubles of a woman named Sherri Finkbine became headline news. Sherri Finkbine was a mother of four, a local television personality who hosted the children's program "Romper Room" in Phoenix, Arizona. While she was pregnant with her fifth child, she had been taking the tranquilizer thalidomide. Then it was revealed publicly that thalidomide when taken during pregnancy caused babies to be born without arms or legs and with other serious birth defects.

When Sherri Finkbine learned this, she reluctantly asked the local hospital board for an abortion. They granted it on the grounds of "suicidal depression." But when she told her story to a local newspaper—so that other pregnant women would be alerted to the dangers of thalidomide—the hospital abortion board, angry at having its inner workings made public, withdrew its approval. This sent Sherri Finkbine on a humiliating public search for an abortion. Reporters and TV crews camped out on her front lawn. She and her husband were both fired from their jobs. Finally, she flew to Sweden for abortion. The aborted fetus was severely deformed.

Carefully watching Sherri Finkbine's troubles were early members of the American women's movement, people such as Gloria Steinem and Betty Friedan, who connected women's difficulties in controlling their own bodies—Margaret Sanger's old slogan—to other kinds of discrimination against women. As "women's liberation," as the movement was called then, gained momentum, reproductive freedom became a major part of it.

In 1965, supporters of women's liberation helped get state laws against selling or giving information about contraception repealed or overturned. In a very important court case called *Griswold* v. *Connecticut*, the U.S. Supreme Court decided that such laws violated the rights of privacy of married couples. This was also an important issue in my court case, *Roe* v. *Wade*, five years later.

By the end of the 1960s several states, including California, New York, and Hawaii, had "reformed" their old abortion laws to make the medical grounds for legal abortions clearer. This usually had the effect of making abortions somewhat easier to obtain.

Naturally, this outraged the Catholic Church and the strict anti-abortionists. They began to organize the so-called "pro-life" movement.

But "pro-choice" activists weren't happy, either. The question of whether an abortion was available to a woman still depended on where she lived and how much money she had. There was no real logic or justice in the situation at all.

The only real solution was a nationwide law that allowed women to make up their own minds. Obviously, something had to be done.

﹏ 5 ﹏

With two short interruptions, I lived in the State School for Girls in Gainesville from age eleven to age fifteen. The three years I spent in reform school were the happiest of my childhood.

It always shocks people when I say this. It even shocks me a little to hear myself saying it! But it's as true as anything I know. I had many friends in reform school, special friends. And I learned important things from them—things, I think, that stayed in the back of my mind and helped me to survive the hard years afterwards.

I made a visit to Gainesville a little while ago, and the sleepy old town looked just the same—like an old-fashioned insurance ad, or an argument against the people who say that the happy families they used to show on television never really existed. Outside the school walls, Gainesville is full of family houses set back from shady, tree-filled streets. Kids toss balls to each other, dogs run free, and men stand on their front lawns with garden hoses in their hand. Although the cars on the street are new, the downtown shops look about thirty years behind the times.

The State School is on the outskirts of town, down a narrow country road and spread out on a grassy hill. If you don't know better, or want to pretend, you might say it looks almost like a junior college. The residents' cottages are light brown, and the superintendent's house, like a little country mansion, is still there right in the middle. A few things have changed over the years, though.

The woman at the guard gate I talked to said that the school first went co-ed, and then—after the gang wars started up about ten years ago—went all male. There aren't that many girl reform school students anymore, she said, and it's too dangerous to mix the sexes. The girls were moved to other schools or put in counseling programs or daytime treatment centers. The boys sentenced to Gainesville these days, she told me, are mostly murderers and rapists, drug addicts and drug dealers.

There is a strong-looking metal fence, maybe twenty feet high and topped with barbed wire and broken glass, around the entire school grounds. When I lived at the State School, there was no fence. There was no guard gate, either. There was just a man every-body called Papa McDowell, an old tobacco-chewing farmer, who sat at the front entrance in the back of his pickup truck. Papa McDowell always carried a rusty old sawed-off shotgun.

"What are you doin' today, Papa?" I'd ask him.

"Keepin' the peace, girl. Just keepin' the peace," he'd say.

Papa McDowall was sitting there when I arrived at the school, and he was still sitting there when I left. He was there to stop the girls from running away. But nobody ever did run away, or even really try. During our free time in the evenings, we talked about how unfair it was that we were all locked up—and how we'd like to walk out the front door, flag down a car, and "go on the free." But when I was alone at night, I would think about it again—and decide that the idea of living back in Dallas scared me more than anything in the school.

In Gainesville I had my own room, with a window, a little radio, and a bookcase and dresser next to my bed. There were twenty rooms, and twenty girls, in each cottage. The cottages were named after women in the Bible: Rebecca, Hannah, Sarah, and so on. Naomi was the Honors Cottage, and I lived there several times. I was also the Junior Mayor of Rebecca. And once, toward the end, I became the only three-time loser to be elected Mayor of Honors Cottage.

At Gainesville we wore our own clothes. The counselors and teachers lived in town or in separate apartments on campus. There was a swimming pool and a ball field, and we'd get taken on trips to town to go to the movies or to the roller-skating rink. The super-

intendent, Mrs. Maxine Birmingham, was a gray-haired lady, not
mean or snooty at all, who lived in a big brick house right in the
middle of the school grounds.

The best girls, and I was sometimes one of them, were given
the best assignment: to help Mrs. Birmingham's maid straighten
her big house up for her. Whenever I was chosen, the maid was
completely drunk on Mrs. Birmingham's cooking sherry, and my
friends and I sat in Mrs. B's big easy chair in the den and watched
TV. For a while, too, I delivered the mail out to the cottages on a
little girl's bicycle with mail sacks on either side of the rear wheel. I
picked up the mail from the administration building and pedaled
it all around the school. I never lost a letter, and I always delivered
everything on time. The other girls were glad to see me, and I
liked that.

The sad fact is that I ran away from my "real" home twice in
order to get back to the school for another nine-month term. And
a lot of the other girls didn't seem to be much different than me.
Most of us, even if we had done crimes, seemed to be there basically because we didn't get along with our parents.

Twice I was released at the end of the school year. Both times,
my mother's then-boyfriend, a truck driver named Raymond, was
living in the house on McKinney Avenue. My father didn't come
around there at all. Most of the time, in fact, I didn't even know
where he was staying. I supposed my parents had other things to
worry about, and I tried to keep that idea in my head, but it made
me angry that nobody had much time or room for me. So both
times I took the bus over to the park near Lake Dallas and slept
there in the open for a few days. The police picked me up. There
were hearings, and they sent me back to Gainesville, saying they
hoped that this time I would learn my lesson. The lesson I learned
was this: I had to watch out for myself, make the best of things, and
try to keep moving until I found a place where the sadness and
anger weren't too bad.

For a while in the beginning, my mother visited me once a
month, a couple of hours each time, talking mostly about how
upset she was that I was in this awful place. When she left I cried,
missing her despite everything, and hating myself for feeling that

way. Then I started worrying about her next visit. My father visited me only once. He sent me a letter to say that he was coming, and on the day he mentioned I waited for him in the visitors' area. I waited most of the day, and he came about an hour before closing time.

"I'm sorry, honey," he said, "I should have left the house a lot earlier." I told him that I was just glad to see him, that it didn't matter he was so late. But I knew I was lying, and so did he.

Gainesville was where I belonged, but it was plain even to me that even though it looked like a regular school, it certainly wasn't. The girls were from all over Texas: white and Hispanic, big and small, blonds, brunettes, redheads, loud and dirty-mouthed, meek and shy. None of us were angels—although almost everyone, on their way to junior prison, had hurt themselves much more than they'd hurt anyone else

Many of the girls were mean, or crazy, or both. Some had actually used guns in robberies. There were fights every day, sometimes with knives stolen from the lunchroom. A couple of the girls tried to kill themselves, by swallowing ground glass or by throwing their plastic radios on the floor and cutting their wrists with pieces of its broken cabinet.

Most of the adults at Gainesville were very strict, and a few were mean and bad-tempered. For breaking the rules—which I did regularly—I was punished. I lost town privileges, and I was given kitchen duty or extra work details. Once, because I secretly mimeographed a pile of handbills asking everyone to join an "I Hate All Adults Club," I was put in the "Meditation Room," by myself, for a week.

But I was almost used to that from Mount St. Michael's. There was a lot of time to daydream in Gainesville, and not all my daydreams were sad ones. Sometimes I'd pretend I had new and different parents: like Mrs. Tuttle, my music class teacher, or Mrs. Estes, my Texas history teacher, or Mrs. Kelling, my upholstery teacher. Or especially Mrs. Wilson, my caseworker for all three years.

During our weekly meetings, which I looked forward to, Mrs. Wilson and I would talk about my favorite courses, photography and science, and I'd tell her how much I'd like to grow up and go to work taking pictures, or maybe study gorillas and other primates in Africa.

"Norma, you've got brains," she'd say. "If you concentrate on one thing you can really get ahead."

Mrs. Wilson was always disappointed when I came back. But although I never had the courage to tell her, she was one of the biggest reasons I always did.

There was another reason. When I was on the outside, in Dallas, I missed my girlfriends, who I loved more than anything in the world. Most of my Gainesville girlfriends were cosmetology students, and they were always doing my hair. "We want to do Norma's hair. It's so pretty and so naturally curly," they said. We necked and kissed and just held each other when we could steal some privacy. A pack of cigarettes would get you an empty room for an hour.

We told each other that since there were no boys around, we had to be boyfriends and girlfriends for each other. I was popular, and I had girlfriends all over the school. I had a campus girlfriend, I had a cottage girlfriend, I had a lunchroom girlfriend. I had a history class old lady. And I was a girlfriend to other girls when that way seemed right. My biggest crush was on Lydia, a Latino girl from San Antonio, who everybody said looked just like me: short, thin, and with dark curly hair.

"*Mi quita*," she called me. My twin.

She taught me a song in Spanish: "*Olvida de Todas,*" which means "Forget Everyone But Me." I loved Lydia very much, and I told her that. I also told her that I was going to marry her and have all her children. Inside the walls of our cottage, just the two of us, it sometimes even seemed possible.

But, of course, it wasn't.

After I turned fifteen, Mrs. Wilson told me that they were going to release me again. But this time, she said sadly, if I messed up I would be sent to another place, more like a prison than a school.

"Do you understand what I'm saying, honey?" she asked. I told her I did.

What I really felt was lonely and afraid and angry. And if I had known what was really going to happen to me I would have risked jail in a second.

When I got back to Dallas Raymond was still living with my mother. Back at Gainesville, my mother and I had talked some about my going back to Louisiana and living with my grandmother. But my mother had a better idea: she wanted to stick by me to help me make something of myself. At last she realized, she said, that it wasn't comfortable for either of us for me to live in the house with her and Raymond. The solution was that I would room in a house near Dallas, with a distant relative of hers, a man who ran a lock-smith shop out of his home. He'd be kind enough to take me in for a very low rent.

I'd never met this relative before. He was a big man, with a last name that sounded Italian. I don't remember it exactly. I suppose I've blocked it out.

The first night I stayed at this man's house he locked up the shop, came up the stairs to my room, climbed into my bed, and forced me to have sex with him. I tried to fight him off, but he was much too powerful. The second night he came back, and then the third. He made me do ugly things to him that, even today, I can't bring myself to write about.

After a few days I stopped fighting. And then I was ashamed of myself for giving in. Much too ashamed to tell anybody or ask anybody for help. Who would believe me? Everybody would laugh in my face. Or worse—much worse—the police would be called in. It would be the man's word against mine, and they'd blame me for accusing him falsely of doing those disgusting things. They would say the sickness and evil had come from my own mind. Then I would go to jail.

So I decided to keep as much control as I could. I stayed awake all night, pulling the covers tight around me, listening. When I heard him coming, I was ready to blank out my mind, to go to another place inside myself, before he turned the doorknob. Some nights I almost succeeded.

In the mornings, after he was gone, I cried and cursed and decided I would have to put up with it until I was eighteen—and when I was an adult, out of the reach of the juvenile court, I would run away to wherever I wanted, as far away from Dallas as it was possible to run.

That seemed to be the only way out. But, thank God, I was

wrong. After three weeks my mother took a good look at me, grabbed my arm and made me tell her why I had dark circles under my eyes. I was too depressed and exhausted to lie or hide anymore, so I told her what was going on.

Completely to my surprise, she didn't blame me for what had happened. Instead, she took me over to the man's house and cussed him out in front of me. She called him a pervert and a criminal and threatened to call the police on him.

The man denied everything. He laughed and—just like in my fears—accused me of making up the whole story. But my mother said she didn't believe him. So he cursed back, shouting and accusing me and calling me and my mother sluts and whores. In the end he threw us out of his house. The matter never went any further than that. Although this man sometimes appears in my nightmares, I never saw him again.

After a lifetime of being raped by this animal, a lot of me seemed to be gone. Even the anger. Even most of the pain. There were certainly no rape counselors in Norma Nelson's world back then. No psychiatrists, either.

So, of course, there were also no answers. There was hardly even a question. Instead, there was a big empty space inside of me, and nightmares.

For the next month I stayed with my mother and Raymond, but even though I was polite to them and she was being nicer to me than usual, doing nothing gave me too much time to think about things. Silence and aloneness were my enemies, I decided. I got a job working full time at Cybil's, a drive-in burger joint not far from where we lived.

I worked as a roller-skating carhop. I skated the orders out to the customers' cars, and I wore a cowgirl outfit: a short skirt with fringe around the edge, a buckskin vest, a cowboy hat, and a holster with two little toy guns.

I was good at being a roller-skating waitress, and when my mind was distracted from my memories, it was almost fun. The other girls were mostly high school students who lived with their parents. During their breaks, they talked about their boyfriends, and how good their boyfriends were in bed, and what they would buy to decorate their new houses when they finally quit this job and got married. Sometimes they teased me for being small and young and boyfriend-less, but they were good to be with—it reminded me, with sweet pain, of Gainesville, although I never told anyone I'd been there.

After a few weeks one of the older girls, Rita, who lived with her father, Jerry, the short order cook at Cybil's, invited me to move in with them in their house across the street. Raymond and my mother seemed relieved.

My world narrowed down to Cybil's and some of my old friends from the neighborhood. Most nights, I could squeeze the past out of my mind and keep the nightmares from coming.

Then, one weekday afternoon, a girl named Deanne skated up to take an order for a car when she wasn't supposed to. In that instant, my entire life changed.

The car she'd waited on had parked in one of my parking slots. So I said to her: "Just for that, girl, I'm going to steal the next car right back from you."

As these words left my mouth a car rolled up: a beautiful '57 Ford Fairlane, jet black. It was nosed, decked, deep-chromed, and waxed until it shone. It had wheel skirts and fancy exhaust pipes. It had a 287-cubic-inch engine, said the numbers written out in chrome on its side.

The driver honked his horn and gunned the motor. I skated over and looked inside. The Fairlane had a custom interior, roll-pleated upholstery, and a dashboard covered completely with car-pet. That car was the prettiest one I had ever seen.

The driver was a small man, almost as short as I was, but he was as handsome as anyone I'd seen outside a Hollywood movie. He had black hair in a pompadour, broad shoulders, and a tiny waist. He was wearing clean dungarees, flip-flop sandals, and a clean white button-down shirt, open at the collar and tied calypso style at the waist.

"What's your name, doll?" he said, in a funny accent.

"What's it to you, mister?" I said. "What do you want?"

"Give me a furburger and a cherry coke," said the man, still talking funny.

"All right, then. That's better," I said, and skated off.

"He wants a furburger and a cherry coke," I told Jerry. The cook's face got very serious.

"Well, honey," he said, "who told you they wanted a furburger?"

"That man in the black car over there."

"Well, go out there and tell him we're fresh out of furburgers," said Jerry. "What else would he like?"

Deanne had skated over out of nowhere. When she heard what we'd been saying, she started to laugh out loud.

"What's your problem?" I said. I didn't know why she was laughing, and it made me mad.

"Norma, how old are you?" she said.

"Almost sixteen."

"Okay, Norma, it's time you knew what a furburger is." She called the other girls over to listen to her tell me.

"Well, you know, Norma," said Deanne, "it's when a guy eats you."

"What?"

"You know, he eats you. Down there. Instead of, you know, the guy letting it happen one way, it happens another way."

I still didn't understand what she was talking about, but the girls were starting to laugh at me again, so I didn't want to let on that I was ignorant.

"Oh, yeah. I understand," I said. I skated back to the black car, not really knowing whether this guy had insulted me, or how badly. I decided to pretend that it didn't matter what he'd said.

"Look, we haven't got any furburgers. What else would you like?"

"I'll have a BLT, doll."

When I placed that order, everybody laughed even more. I decided I would show them I wasn't as young or stupid as they thought I was. But how?

"What time to you get off, doll?" said the man when I placed the tray in his car window.

"I'm not getting in that car with you, mister," I said.

But he just smiled. Not a bad smile, I thought.

When closing time came around he was still parked in the same spot. His car was still beautiful. I hated those girls for laughing at me. And every one of them except me had a boyfriend. After my shift was over, I walked toward my apartment. When I passed the Ford Fairlane, the man jumped out of his seat and opened the door on the passenger side. For me.

I shook my head, folded my arms, glared back over my shoulder at the other girls, and slid in.

We drove off down the road to nowhere in particular. He told me about himself. I mostly listened. His name was Woody McCorvey. Ellwood Blanchfield McCorvey the Third. He was twenty-four. Not a boy anymore, I thought. He was a man. His skin was whiter than any man's I'd seen. I imagined the tops of mountains in Alaska were that white.

The reason he talked so funny, saying "youse" instead of "you" and "seen" instead of "saw" was that he was from Upstate New York.

"From Buffalo, New York. You can't get much more upstate than that," he said. Buffalo was where his mother, who was Italian, still lived. His father, who had moved down to Texas, owned a sheet metal shop over in Pasadena, near Houston.

"I can work for my father anytime," said Woody, "but I'm out here in Dallas looking for a job on my own."

He was free as a bird, he said. He was a sheet metal worker, a man with a trade. He was starting all over. He'd been married once, but he wasn't anymore.

"There was something wrong with her insides. She couldn't give me any children. So it didn't work out."

He didn't say anything else for a while. We just cruised through the neighborhood. The car drove smoothly, at the same time making a great noise from its exhaust pipes.

Woody leaned back in his seat, steering with one hand. People stared at us from the sidewalk, and from other cars.

He pulled into a gas station, gave the attendant two dollars, and told him fill up the tank.

"Nice car, buddy," said a man filling up at another pump.

I was excited to be riding in such a fine car with Woody, although I tried not to let on. That night, Woody dropped me off. The next night, he did the same, and the third night he pulled up in front of his motel.

"Norma, I want to sleep with you," he said to me.

It seems strange to say this, but I had never before heard anyone use that term before. I imagined the two of us together in a bed, just sleeping.

"Okay," I said, a little puzzled. He smiled, took me inside, and showed me exactly what he meant.

After that, Woody McCorvey was my boyfriend. When they found this out, the other girls stopped teasing me and we had more to talk about. I was glad of both these things.

Woody spent his days looking for work, or at least he said he did, and picked me up every night at Cybil's when my shift was over. Woody bought us dinner there, then drove us back to his motel, and then, after a few hours, drove me home.

Unlike a lot of the other girls' boyfriends, Woody didn't drink or take drugs. In those early days, he didn't even get angry or hit me.

He did like to have sex, though, and although I liked the closeness and having him hold me before and afterwards, I couldn't figure out why the other girls said they enjoyed the actual sex part so much. Sometimes, having sex with Woody brought up bad memories. It also hurt me, physically, inside. I was too shy and confused to bring up the subject with him. Finally, I figured that in exchange for having Woody, I would just have to put up with it. Having Woody as a boyfriend was much better than being alone. He loved me. I was fairly sure of that. Sometimes we even spent the entire night together. One morning, Woody listened to me singing along with a song on the radio, and he told me that I had a great singing voice and that with a little practice and meetings with the right people I would be able to get a record contract from RCA. He would be my manager, and I would be famous and we would both get rich. He knew all about that kind of thing, he said.

I didn't believe him, not really, but just the thought of it sounded exciting.

There were moments, before it all fell apart, when I believed I could genuinely love Woody McCorvey forever. One thing in particular made me feel closer to him: he was the only man I'd ever met who talked about his dreams.

"Now, I don't want you to think I'm funny or anything," he'd say, smoking a cigarette. Then he would tell me all he could remember.

"I dreamed about two flowers all tangled up together," he told me one day. "And then there would be four flowers, and eight flowers, and so on and so on."

Or sometimes he would talk about a dream that he often had, about people dancing together in a green pasture, wearing long shiny dresses.

"What do you think it means, doll?" he asked me.

"I don't know, sweetie."

I thought back to the magic and the dream signs I'd learned back in Lettesworth. But the strange thing was that they were no help for what he'd told me. No help at all.

After a few months the girls at Cybil's began to tease me again, asking me when Woody and I were going to get married. They kept it up for so long that after awhile it stopped being just a joke. I began to wonder, too.

Maybe, I thought, this is what I felt was missing. Maybe living together in our own house, as man and wife with our own children, would bring me the kind of pleasure that everybody else talked about.

But Woody never talked about getting married—only about how nasty and selfish and unsexy and barren his ex-wife was. I wondered how to bring up the subject, but I couldn't figure out a way to do it.

Then one night, surprising even myself, I did. Woody had driven us to the motel, just like always, and opened his door to get out. But I just sat in the car.

"Come on, doll," he said.

"No," I said in a low voice.

"Now, Norma, what's wrong with you? Come on in inside with me."

"No," I said in a louder voice.

"Why not?" he said.

I told him I was tired. That I wasn't in the mood.

But neither of those two things were true, I realized. Or any more true than it ever was. An idea that I hadn't even known I'd had was forming in my brain.

"I don't want to do this anymore. But I want to be married."

Woody stood still for a second, stunned. And then he grinned. "Aw, come on, Norma. What are you saying to me?"

"I want you to marry me. Then I'll go inside."

For the next half-hour he joked and pleaded, trying to get me out of his car, but he finally gave up and drove me home.

For the next few days I wouldn't even ride in his car with him. Only if he agreed to marry me, I said.

I half-expected him to give up and go away—and part of me, I realize now, was hoping he would. But a few days of no sex later, Woody said he would marry me.

It was one of the worst mistakes I've ever made. I did it with no more thought than I'd give now to a new sofa or a set of tires.

On our wedding day we drove downtown to the courthouse. Woody wore what he was wearing the first day I met him: dungarees and a white shirt, tied calypso style, and flip-flops. I wore a black long-sleeved blouse and black stretch pants.

We found out that one particular judge, the Honorable Joe E. Brown, was doing weddings that day, and after only a little bit of a wait he married us, between trials, in his chambers. It only took a few minutes, and cost only a few dollars.

"Are you happy now, doll?" said Woody, and I told him I was.

I had just turned sixteen. My mother had to sign permission for me to get married, but after that, I figured, I was a grownup, free to do whatever I wanted to with my life.

If any two people in the history of the world had no business being married, it was Woody McCorvey and me. I haven't seen my ex-husband, the father of my daughter, in more than twenty years. The last information I heard, he was an itinerant metal worker—a drifter who only gets in touch with his family when he is out of money or in other kinds of trouble.

As for myself, I also lived for a time as a drifter, out of touch with my family and most of normal society. And I know now that loving and marrying a man, even a kind and gentle man, which Woody was not, is not in my nature. But all this was in a future I could not then even begin to imagine.

On June 17, 1964, I became Mrs. Woody McCorvey. That wasn't the only change: my new husband and I decided that now that we were married, we'd have to give up our old dreams and look for our fortune in a new way. The first step, Woody said, was for him to stop looking for work in Dallas and settle back down with his father in Pasadena.

It sounded like a good idea. Because only God knew, judging from Woody's experience, how hard it was for a good sheet metal worker to find employment in Dallas those days. I quit my job, said good-bye to everybody at Cybil's, and we drove to Houston in the black Ford. It was our last long ride together in that beautiful car.

I'm not quite sure even today whether Woody told his parents ahead of time that we'd gotten married, or that he was coming to see them. Whatever the truth was, there seemed more of a tangled history between Woody and his parents then he'd let on.

When we got to Pasadena, Woody's mother refused to let me into her house until I showed her my marriage license. Mr. McCorvey, Woody's dad, seemed glad to see us, although, to say the least, he wasn't as enthusiastic as I'd expected about the idea of his son going back to work for him. Mrs. McCorvey told me that she was very concerned about the sleeping arrangements—so concerned that she told me I had to sleep on the living room couch. I had to beg and plead and yell back at her, just like at my own mother, to get her to let us sleep together in Woody's old bedroom.

We lived with the McCorveys for two weeks. During that time, Woody somehow never got it together enough to go back to work in his father's shop. He woke up around noon, got out of bed and got dressed, and drove his mother around town on her errands. In the evenings there were arguments, with everyone screaming and yelling and crying—mainly about me and what was I doing with Woody and how long were we staying.

After a week or so of this I began spending most of my time in the garage, listening to the radio. Mrs. McCorvey heard me singing along with it once, and in one of the few complimentary things she ever said to me, told me that I had a lovely singing voice. Just like Woody had back in the motel. When I told Woody this, he had his big new idea. Or rather, he said, it was an old idea that he'd been thinking about for some time.

Working with sheet metal would always be there for him, Woody told me. The important thing was that we give our biggest dreams a chance.

"Why don't we move to Los Angeles, which is where Hollywood is, and give you a shot at a singing career?" said Woody.

Here was how he had figured it: as my manager and press agent, he would get me started in the recording business. Then, when my career really got going, he would take a little bit of the money that I made, rent an old building in Hollywood, and set up a sheet metal shop for himself to run.

"You know, darlin'," he said to me, "by the time I get that shop going, you'll have two or three gold records already. We'll have plenty of money. Then you won't have to work at all. It's a perfect plan.

No it wasn't. Even a sixteen-year-old married woman knew that.

At first, the idea of me as a singing star seemed as crazy to me as it does now. But Woody kept talking about it, even in front of his parents, who didn't know much about the music business but didn't have anything to say against the plan at all. After a few days, despite my better judgment, I began to believe it was possible, just a little bit. Then Woody surprised me with another idea: to fund the beginning of our life in Los Angeles, he would sell his car. Yes, he said, he would actually do that.

I couldn't say no to a man who had picked me out from among all the girls in Texas and could believe in me like that. That car was the most beautiful thing in our lives—and Woody was willing to give it up for our dream. We both cried when the new owner drove it away. Woody's parents drove us to the train station, and two and a half days later, sitting up and hardly sleeping all the way, we arrived in Los Angeles.

It did feel like a dream, in a way. Taking a bus marked "HOLLY-WOOD" from the train station, we somehow arrived at a place called Barris Custom City, a big showroom filled with customized hot rods, like Woody's Ford, except they were bigger and much fancier.

There were little signs saying what movies the cars had been in, and that they had been driven by stars like Bobby Darin and Sandra Dee. For hours, it seemed, we stood around that show-room, pointing out to each other all the little details on the cars and how we would have customized the cars a little differently. Thinking back, this might have been the happiest time in our entire marriage. It makes me sad to remember it.

Then we walked and walked—for miles and miles, it seemed. We wound up at Grauman's Chinese Theater, and we put our hands and feet into the old stars' concrete handprints and foot-prints, just like all the other tourists. I was very tired after that, but what I remember best is walking on Hollywood Boulevard past a raggedy little newsstand, covered completely with newspapers hung on it with clothespins.

"RUDOLPH VALENTINO DEAD" read the headline on every one of those newspapers.

I suddenly remembered something: my mother had once told me that Rudolph Valentino was her favorite actor. It struck me so hard that he had died that I began to cry.

"What's the matter?" said Woody.

"Did he die suddenly?" I asked the man running the newsstand. The man grinned and told me that Rudolph Valentino had died a long time ago. These were souvenir newspapers, he explained, and for a dollar, I could get one with any headline I wanted.

Actually, a lot of things in Hollywood weren't exactly what they appeared to be. Although it was supposed to be a glamorous and exciting place, just about all we could see of Hollywood looked seedy. There weren't any movie studios or recording studios that we could find, only a lot of flimsy-looking apartment houses and liquor stores. After dark, Hollywood just looked dangerous.

After two nights in a motel, which ate up most of the money in our pockets, and a couple of days walking the streets looking for any kind of an apartment we could afford, we wound up in front of a wood-frame rooming house on the outskirts of Hollywood. I was tired and homesick and hungry. "Sir, do you have any rooms?" I asked an old man sitting on the front porch.

"Where are you from, little girl?" he said.

"Texas."

"Well, then, say 'Howdy' for me."

"Howdy."

"Yep, you're from Texas," he said. Then he sighed, stretched, and got up and showed us the last room he had available.

From the outside, the rooming house didn't look much different from anything you'd see in a poor part of Dallas or Houston. But inside were people who were different from us. They were people our age: early hippies, the men with long hair in ragged jeans and T-shirts, the women with even longer hair, combed straight down to their waists, in flowing dresses and peasant shirts. They interested me—I thought of the beatniks in the coffee shop back in Dallas—but they also scared me, because they were so strange. I didn't talk to them unless I had to.

Lying down in our little room, listening to the strange music they played, and the strange—and complicated—rock and roll music that poured into the streets from radios and record players all over Hollywood, the idea of hooking up with the recording industry seemed more hopeless than ever.

Woody did say that he'd made a couple of calls to music stores about me. All he would say about them was that he hadn't gotten in touch with RCA just yet. Then he stopped talking about my recording career altogether.

I stopped asking about it, too. Woody's mood seemed to change for the worse as the days dragged by. He got very quiet, except when he was angry at me. I also got angry back at him sometimes, although mostly I think I was just plain scared.

Woody began leaving the rooming house early each morning. He was hitting the streets, he said, to look for work. There was no sense in me looking for a job. At sixteen, I was too young even to buy a pack of cigarettes in the state of California. Most days, Woody didn't come home until well after dark. That left me alone to shop for food and keep the room clean.

We were broke. Woody called his father collect and persuaded him to wire us some emergency money. After two weeks, that money almost completely ran out. Then, just as I was feeling really desperate—I could run away, I thought over and over, but to where?—Woody came home one afternoon with a surprise.

"Doll, I got myself a job," he said. Which was good—because by that time I was feeling worse than just homesick. Although I hadn't bothered Woody with my problem yet, I was feeling sick to my stomach a lot, too.

Woody had been hired to work in a sheet metal factory in a place called El Monte. El Monte was a town about twenty miles east of Hollywood. On the map it was just a little spot near no place I had ever heard of, where three freeways came together. Somehow, Woody scraped together enough money to buy a 1956 Oldsmobile, a big green monster with bald tires and a 357-cubic-inch engine.

We packed our suitcase again and moved to El Monte. It turned out to be a town almost as flat as Houston, full of junkyards and used car lots and drive-in movies. We rented a tiny apartment in a pink stucco building that wasn't a motel but was built just like one. We had a tiny bathroom, a tiny kitchen, and a room with a fold-out sofabed. Woody left each morning, taking the Oldsmobile with him. And I could not shake off my stomach bug. I was still feeling sick.

I was as lonely as I'd ever been. During the daytime, the only one around was the manager, a middle-aged woman named Ruth. Ruth was friendly—she looked a little lonely herself—and I got to tell her about myself and Woody. After a few days, I told her my secret: I felt sick to my stomach, my breasts were sore, and I had to go to the bathroom a lot.

Ruth put her hand over her mouth. "Oh my God, honey," she said. "You're pregnant."

I was surprised. More than surprised. Shocked. And when some of the shock wore off, I was frightened and ashamed of my own ignorance. I had a vague idea of how babies were made—the girls back in Gainesville talked about it—but nobody older had ever actually sat me down and told me for certain. Somehow, what Woody and I had been doing together didn't seem to be what was needed to create a whole new life.

Of course that was wrong, I thought. How stupid could one person be?

When Ruth's voice came into focus again, she was looking into the phone book and giving me the address of the nearest free medical clinic. It wasn't far away.

I didn't say anything to Woody when he came home that night. The next morning, I took the bus to the clinic address and sat in the waiting room with the other patients. There were no men. Just women and children. Some of the women looked nearly as scared as I felt.

It wasn't until late in the afternoon that the doctor could see me. I told him what I had been going through. He examined me, told me to put my clothes back on, and said that yes, I might be pregnant. "But without a urine sample," he said to me, "I really can't tell."

"Okay," I said, and quickly left the examining room.

I didn't know what a urine sample was because I didn't know what urine was, and I was afraid of what getting a sample of it could

mean—would it hurt?—and I was afraid that I would show my ignorance by asking.

So I decided to just take it for granted that I was pregnant. I
walked all the way home, my mind flooded with the brand-new
idea of having a baby with Woody. Did I really want to have children with him? Were we really a family? I looked deep down into
myself and the answer scared me. All I could see was unhappiness
and disappointment. Maybe even worse.

But I pushed those terrible thoughts away. I was going to have a
baby, I said to myself. There was nothing to do about it. I would
have to turn us, somehow, into the kind of family we needed to be.

A picture of a happy family having dinner—I'd seen one in a
magazine advertisement in the waiting room—popped into my
head. On the way home I shopped as carefully as I ever had for
food: I bought a Chef Boy-R-Dee spaghetti dinner, about thirty-
cents' worth of chopped beef, and a small head of lettuce.

I had about a dollar left, so I a bought a red-and-white-checked
gingham tablecloth. When I got home I made the lettuce into a
make-believe salad, cooked the meat and mixed in some tangy
ketchup to make spaghetti sauce, and put the tablecloth on our
kitchen table. I picked some wildflowers from the front lawn, put
then into an empty pop bottle, and set the table with the flowers in
the center. Then I sat down and waited for Woody to come home.

He did, in an hour or so. He was sweaty and dirty from the factory job, and since he didn't like to talk until he was showered and
changed—sometimes he'd curse and clench his fists when I
annoyed him—I didn't say anything until he sat down. I spooned
out his dinner and he started to eat.

"Guess what I did today, Woody?" I said. "I went down to the
free clinic and they said I could possibly be pregnant."

At first, Woody didn't speak. He just sat there eating. Finally, he
looked up at me.

"So what did you do today, doll?" he said.

"I went down to the free clinic and they said I could possibly be
pregnant." This time it was even harder to say.

Woody put down his fork and smiled a strange smile.

"Oh, no," he said. "That's not so. You couldn't be that. We're
having too much fun."

"I know we are," I said. Then I went all the way back to the beginning, telling him about my sick stomach, my talk with Ruth, and my visit to the doctor. As I told him this I saw him getting angry, very angry, but I felt that it was too late to stop. I just had to get it all out.

That was a bad mistake. Just as the thought reached me that he was angrier than I'd ever seen him, he reached out, grabbed my hair, and yanked my face toward him. Then he slapped my face, hard.

"How could you do this?" he yelled.

"What do you mean?" I said, still stunned by his hitting me.

"I can't get women pregnant! None of my wives got pregnant! I didn't get you pregnant! It's not fucking mine!"

For a second, I didn't understand what he was saying. Then, horribly, I did.

"It is yours, Woody. I swear it is. It's yours."

"Bitch! Liar!" Then he slapped me again. And again and again, maybe five times, maybe ten. Pain began to penetrate the shock.

I put my hands over my face, blocking his slaps. He grabbed me by the shoulders and threw me against the kitchen wall. I slumped to the floor, but he picked me up, punched me, and threw me into the living room, against the edge of the couch.

He was screaming the same words over and over again. I was crying and cursing him back.

Then he stopped for a little while to catch his breath. For some reason he kept away from me long enough for me to drag myself into the bathroom and lock the door. My stomach began to hurt, worse than it ever had. Woody banged and pounded on the door and shook the doorknob until I wondered if the flimsy lock would hold.

"Go away! Go away!" I yelled. "I hate you, fucker! I never want to see you again!"

After a few more minutes of banging and yelling and threatening me, he stopped, and I heard what sounded like him stomping out and slamming the door behind him. I waited a half-hour until I was sure, then unlocked the door and stumbled to the couch.

The feelings I had then, of shame and pain and anger and panic, are still horrible to remember.

* * *

After an hour or two, maybe, there was a knock on the door. I flinched and started for the bathroom.

"Norma, it's me," said Ruth.

I dragged myself off the couch and let her in.

"Oh, my God! What happened?" she said.

"We had a fight. He hurt me pretty bad," I said.

"Is he coming back?" she asked.

I nodded, crying.

Then Ruth noticed that Woody had left his keys on the kitchen table. "I'm going to lock all your windows. I want you to double lock your door." She gave me a wet towel to put on my head, then left.

I pulled open the bed, lay down on it, and cried myself to sleep.

I woke up in the dark to the sound of glass breaking. A black shape was coming through the living room window. Without thinking I grabbed something heavy, I don't remember what, and moved toward the thing coming toward me. For a split second I looked into Woody's eyes and then I moved to hit him. I don't know whether I managed to do it or not.

I didn't feel anything when he hit me in the head. The next thing I knew I was on the floor, and someone was standing over me.

"Look," said a man's voice, "she's coming back to us."

I opened my eyes all the way and saw Woody's face. I screamed. Then Woody's face dissolved and it was a policeman, instead.

I stopped screaming. Ruth was standing there, too. The cop and his partner lifted me back onto the bed and asked me my name, and Woody's, and where I thought he had gone to.

I told him I didn't know. That seemed to be a signal to them that they were finished with me. They wrote down their police station's phone number and told me to call them if I saw my husband, and then they left.

I looked through the broken window and realized that it was the next morning. I had been knocked unconscious, said Ruth. She had noticed the door was open and found me.

"Thank you," I said.

I was numb. The bruises on my face didn't hurt, although somewhere underneath, where I could still feel something, I felt a terrible pain. I asked Ruth to leave me alone for a while. I took a shower, because I felt very dirty. Then I changed my clothes and knocked on Ruth's door.

"Can I use your telephone?" I asked her.

I called my mother collect and told her in as few words as possible that I was pregnant, that Woody had hit me, and that I would try to come home. Ruth took the phone to talk to her. I went back inside and packed my clothes.

Ruth shouted through the door: "I found someone who wants to buy your car. Do you have anything else to sell?"

"No," I said, and in an hour she came back and handed me a roll of cash. She put me in her car and drove me over the freeways to Los Angeles Airport. She'd made a plane reservation for me, she said, and she told me I should go to the counter and buy my ticket. Then she hugged me, told me to watch out for myself, and crying, she left.

I did what Ruth had told me to but the lady at the ticket counter told me I'd missed my flight. The next one was in four hours. This was the first time I'd ever ridden in an airplane. Sitting there in the terminal, waiting, I remembered that I'd been afraid of flying. But for some reason, I wasn't frightened of it anymore.

6

In June 1965, the same month I married Woody McCorvey, another Texas woman was changing her life. The woman's name was Sarah Weddington. Although Sarah was only a couple of years older than me, she had already graduated from college and was in Austin, the state capital, preparing to enter the University of Texas law school.

Sarah Weddington was born in Abilene, a small city west of Dallas. She was the daughter of a Methodist minister and grew up in the small towns where he was the preacher. That is all I know about Sarah's family. In *A Matter of Choice*, Sarah's autobiography, neither her mother nor father's first or last name is given.

Unlike me, Sarah was a straight-A student who never got in trouble. She was so smart and hardworking, in fact, that she skipped two grades in school. She was a high school student leader—president of the Future Homeowners of America. But, she writes, despite all her success she always had the inner feeling that she was different, that the goals of the majority of people were not her goals.

Sarah wasn't interested in having children or raising a family. What she was interested in was becoming an attorney. At the time such a profession for a woman was almost unheard of. Her teachers and other adults tried to talk her out of it, but Sarah held on to her dream.

Sarah graduated from McMurry College in Abilene with a

degree in teaching. At the University of Texas, she was one of only five women in her law school class of 120. One of the other women was Linda Coffee, from Houston, who would be her partner during most of the biggest case of her life. At the university she also met Ron Weddington, a fellow student who became her boyfriend.

As a young lawyer, she would represent me in court. Afterwards, she would argue *Roe* v. *Wade* in front of the United States Supreme Court and become a heroine of the women's movement. But back in the middle 1960s, neither of us had the slightest notion that anything like that would happen.

At the end of her second year in law school Sarah Weddington was ranked in the top quarter in her class. But because she was a woman, no major law firm would offer her a job for after graduation. At the beginning of her third and last year in law school she had a bigger problem, however. Her boyfriend Ron was just starting law school himself, she was still unmarried, and she was pregnant.

7

When I got back to Dallas after my beating, I was numb. I spent the first few days in my old room at my mother's house. Those days went by without my feeling much of anything. The months in Hollywood, in El Monte, in California—my whole marriage—seemed like a bad dream, or a bad movie. Only Woody hitting me seemed real. That was because I could feel the bruises he gave me, see them every morning in the mirror. Watching them ripen and darken and then fade away, I tried to tell myself: when they fade away altogether I can forget about it all, put the last six months behind me, and get on with my life.

But after the first week at home the numbness wore off. All my emotions came back with a rush—the fear, the hopelessness, the sadness, all at once.

Worst was the anger. It was an anger deeper and more dangerous than any I'd ever felt. Late at night, and in the morning when I woke up, it tore at my insides and made me tremble with its power. Anger grew inside me like a fist. Other times, it felt like a vicious snake. I wanted it to escape from my body and kill Woody.

No. I wanted to kill Woody. I wanted to kill him for thinking I had cheated on him. I wanted to kill him for hurting me. And what was even more frightening, I wanted to kill him before he or any other person could hurt me again.

Which meant, I realized, that in order to keep from killing Woody, or anyone, I had to be on my guard. If I had the slightest inkling that a person would hurt me, I couldn't trust them—or even take my eyes off them—for an instant.

I had to get on with my life. I went to a free clinic in Dallas and had a urine test—my mother explained to me beforehand what urine was—and found out that I was definitely pregnant. That was nothing more than I knew already. In fact, I felt that my baby was my best friend in my fight for self-control. Even though it was Woody's, it was also mine, and I knew I had enough love left inside of me—it cut right through the anger, even during the worst of times—to love it and be a mother to it and raise it by myself.

At first, at least, my mother agreed with me completely. To my surprise, she wasn't angry at me for making a mess of my marriage. Or getting pregnant. Actually, she said, the fact that I was married when I got pregnant made almost everything all right.

"Bad marriages happen," she said. "It's awful that your life is going the way it's going, but you just have to dig deep down and get things going in the right direction. Do you want to keep this baby?"

"Yes," I told her.

"Do you want to divorce Woody?"

"Yes," I told her.

"All right, then," she said.

She took me downtown and we filed the divorce papers. She also called the police station and got a court order against Woody coming near me.

That was good. Because when Woody got back to Dallas, from wherever he'd gone, he called me.

"Hey, doll! Here I am," he said, as if nothing had happened. But something had happened, and all I felt after I picked up the phone was anger—and fear. I kept myself together enough to lie that my mother had already called the police and if he showed up at our house he would be arrested. But he came over anyway, in a car that I'd never seen before.

Through the front window, I saw him coming up the walk. I forced back all the hundreds of bad feelings flooding over me, ran back into the dining room, and called the police for real.

"Open up, doll!" he shouted through the door. "I'm sorry, honey. Let's go for a ride. Don't you want to go for a ride with me?" he said, as if my locking the door against him was some kind of joke.

"Go away, Woody!" I shouted back. "I'm not married to you anymore. I don't have to listen. Go away!"

He just kept laughing and sweet-talking. Then the police car pulled up. While the cops walked toward him, Woody pounded on the door until the whole house shook. "What are you doing? What are you doing? Let me in! Let me in!" he screamed. "You called the cops on me? You called the fucking cops on me?"

I sat down on the hallway floor, rolled up into a ball and put my hands over my ears to wait until the shouting stopped. They put handcuffs on Woody and took him away to jail. They left his car parked in front of my mother's house. I just stared at it, shaking. A few days later, we had it towed away.

I got a job at Pete's Restaurant, just down the street, the same place where my mother had worked before me. Pete's was open twenty-four hours. I was a waitress on the late shift.

From 11 P.M. to 2 A.M. I served food, sometimes very badly and clumsily because of my new belly, with another girl. I also worked the bar, pouring drinks for the serious drinkers who came in at those hours. Sometimes, to push down the sadness, I poured myself a drink, too.

From 2 to 6 A.M. I was the only waitress. The only people I saw were Scott, the night manager, the cook, and whatever few customers staggered in off the street that late. After midnight, Scott was gone for hours at a time on mysterious errands. Around 3:30 in the morning, the trucks carrying food for the next day arrived. I was usually the only one there to sign for it. I didn't want to get myself or anybody else into trouble, so I signed the invoices "Scott, Manager."

Being pregnant turned out to be both a plus and a minus at Pete's. On the minus side, the cooking smells floating out from the kitchen often made me feel sick. On the plus side, the customers— especially the drinkers— seemed especially fascinated by my pregnancy. Looking at me helped cheer them up. For them, the jokes they told about pregnant women were always hilarious. On the other hand, a future mother seemed to be the right kind of person to tell their troubles to. The tips, particularly when I could bring myself to listen to their hard luck stories and complaints against the world, were very good.

*   *   *

I decided early on that the tip money would be just for the baby. It would go for the doctor and the hospital room, for baby clothes and a baby bed. So I stashed all my tips in a big pickle jar I set at the end of the bar. Each morning at the end of my shift, I brought the jar home and emptied all the money into my dresser drawer.

Raymond, my mother's boyfriend, helped out also. One morning, when he'd just come off the road, he asked me what the money in the jar was for. I told him.

"Well, Norma, how much do you think you've got in that jar?" he asked.

"Ten dollars," I said, and Raymond reached into his pocket and told me he felt like putting ten dollars into the jar himself.

After that, Raymond matched the money in my jar whenever he ran into me. His kindness pushed my long-range planning even further along. During quiet times at the restaurant I'd figured it out: when I came out of the hospital with my baby, I would owe nobody anything. Then we could both start our new lives free and clear. Just the two of us, together.

Unfortunately for me and my unborn baby, the plan turned out to be just a teenager's sad daydream. It started coming apart even as I dreamt it: in the evenings, when Raymond was on the road, my mother always got restless.

When my mother felt restless, she liked to go out and visit the local night spots. One Friday night, my night off, she decided to go to a bar on Haskell Street called Sue's. Things were so good between us that she asked me to come along.

She hadn't been to Sue's in awhile, she said, but she'd heard a crazy thing about it: the bar's new owners had glued egg cartons to the ceiling. "Can you imagine that?" she said. "Norma, I'm going to have to take you down and let you see this." Sue's did have egg cartons glued to the ceilings. They didn't look bad, actually, up there through the darkness and smoke and jukebox music. We sat at the bar and had our drinks, and we talked to the bartender, a woman named Valerie Johnson.*

Valerie Johnson was as big as Mount Everest, but friendly, with a nice smile, and after a little while I told her about myself, including what Woody had done to me.

Then she told me her life story. Or, at least as much as you could tell when you were working in a noisy bar. She was a school-teacher during the week, but she worked at Sue's to make extra money. She wasn't married. But, she said with a laugh, she was looking.

Valerie told me a few jokes, and when it was my turn to talk, she listened carefully. I liked her, and with a little help from the liquor, I told her so.

When I told her I liked her Valerie looked at me closely, as though she were seeing me for the first time. I could see in her eyes that she was coming to some kind of decision.

"Well, you know, Norma," she said, "you need to come back and see us some night. You know, some other night when you're not working."

"Okay," I said. "Maybe I will."

For some reason, my mother thought that was funny. "Come on, Norma, let's get out of here," she laughed. She finished her drink, bottoms up. Then she drove me, weaving through the traffic lanes a little bit, right home.

It was lonely working all by myself at Pete's. For that reason, I supposed, Valerie's friendliness—and how comfortable I felt at Sue's—stayed in my mind. About a month later, on another Friday night off, I went back to Sue's by myself. At first I couldn't get in. A woman carding people at the door, who hadn't been there the last time, told me I was underage.

"Let me talk to Valerie," I said to her.

She looked at me again, more closely this time. "Did Valerie say it was all right for you to come on back?"

"Yes," I said. "I can't get into any trouble here. I'm already pregnant."

She laughed. "Oh, well, then. You must be okay." To my relief, Valerie did remember me. She was even glad to see me.

But this time Sue's looked different. For one reason in particular: it was filled entirely with women. Most of them were dressed casually in jeans or work clothes, and only a few had their hair teased or wore makeup. They were certainly different than the women you'd see in Lilly's Lounge. After working at Pete's, it was strange to be in a bar with no men in it, but everybody seemed to be having a good time anyway, or maybe because of it, playing pool and dancing and talking.

Valerie introduced me to some of the regulars, who were also her friends. They were glad to meet me, and I found I could talk easily to them. None of them talked about their boyfriends or husbands or jobs. They talked about playing softball, or partying, or what their girlfriends had said or done. They seemed different, more relaxed, than any of the women I knew.

After awhile, it began to hit me why I was feeling so good. The place reminded me a little bit of the old coffee house, but even more it reminded me of Gainesville, when I was popular and smart and had lots of girlfriends.

I didn't leave until closing time.

On my next night off I went back to Sue's, and made two new girlfriends myself.

Liz Gilliam* was a cowgirl, Texas born and bred. She had two kids. She was small, like me, and she wore jeans and cowboy boots and a belt with her name engraved on the back. "So I won't forget it," she said. I was sure she's made that joke a thousand times, but it made me laugh anyway.

For some reason, the thick eyeglasses Liz Gilliam wore only made her cuter. The moment I saw her, I knew I wanted to spend the rest of my life with her. Her friend Glennis Long,*, whom she lived with in Fort Worth, was a delivery room nurse. Glennis Long was tall and thin.

I thought it was quite a coincidence, me meeting Glennis Long at Sue's when I was halfway into the delivery room myself. That first night, she told me that sometimes her old patients walked up to her and asked: "Oh hi, Glennis. Do you remember me?"

Liz grinned. She'd heard that one before, too.

"I always tell 'em," said Glennis, "to pull up their dress and pull down their panties. Then their names always come back to me."

Sue's, of course, was a lesbian bar. That's what its new owners had turned it into. At the time, it was one of the few gay women's bars in Dallas—maybe in all of Texas.

Although it may sound a little odd, it's important to say that nobody in that place ever said the word *lesbian*. And I certainly couldn't have told you, those first nights at Sue's, what a lesbian was. Much less tell you that I was one.

All I knew then was that I belonged with these other women. They were different from everybody else, in the same ways that I was different. We were women who loved women. But we weren't there just for sex, though certainly love and sex were a big part of it. What we all were, because we were lesbians, were outsiders. Together.

In the big world, being an outsider was a problem. Inside the bar, though, we could shut out that world.

The sad truth was that a lot of the shutting out had to do with the beer and liquor everybody drank just about all the time. But I didn't realize that until much later. Back then, this secret world was new and exciting.

For me, the new world also included the men's gay bars in Dallas. There were more of them around than anyone ever imagined. They were connected to Sue's in some way I could never figure out—except that the women who worked at Sue's seemed to know all about them.

Maybe they were secretly owned by the same people. Maybe not. There was the White Carriage, the Left Bank, the Gilded Cage. Every single one of them is gone now. My favorite was called the Numbers, on Harwood. It was there that Valerie sent me, just to check it out, when I got a little sad to see Liz and Glennis together, and a little tired of all the same women at Sue's.

The Numbers is long gone now, also, but it was always filled with gentle men who were always glad to talk to a woman. Especially a pregnant woman. The regular customers fussed all over me and made sure I had a comfortable seat and a free Coke.

I made great friends with Louis,[*] the bartender. Louis was a small man, generous and kind and much more feminine than I was then or would ever be. He was well educated and had traveled around the world. He liked to talk to me for hours about the books he'd read and the plays he'd seen and the beautiful cities, like San Francisco, he'd lived in. I didn't always understand the things he was talking about, but I was glad he liked to tell them to me.

The sad part of Louis's life was that his mother, whom he'd loved very much, had died very young. His love affairs—the way his boyfriends would always break up with him—were very sad also. But Louis loved me, too. I knew that. It didn't matter that he liked to sleep with men instead of women.

When I got too pregnant to fit into any of my old clothes, Louis went out and bought me a new pink maternity dress, with matching purse and shoes. They were the prettiest things I owned. Then he bought us two tickets for *Swan Lake,* his favorite ballet, which was playing at Fair Lawn Park in Dallas.

He explained the whole story to me, about the black swan and the white swan, before we went to see it. And when we did see it, it was the most beautiful thing I'd ever seen.

When I was eight months pregnant, I got so big and my ankles got so swollen that I had to quit my job at Pete's. Maternity leave wasn't exactly a policy there, even if I'd known enough to ask for it.

A week later, when I was standing at the bar talking to Louis, my water broke. He called a cab and I went from the Numbers to Dallas Osteopathic Hospital, where my doctor practiced, just like I'd planned. They gave me a shot that paralyzed me from the waist down. I probably didn't need it, because my new daughter was born after only two hours of labor.

After they brought me back to my room they put her in my arms. She was tiny, beautiful, perfect. I was exhausted, and aching, but very happy. I imagined our whole lives—me working hard to make something of myself, the two of us growing up together.

My mother and Raymond visited me. Louis sent over an arrangement of miniature carnations set in real beer cans, signed "From the Gang at the Numbers."

The next day, right after they brought my baby to me for her feeding, Woody McCorvey walked through the door. When I looked up from her and saw his face, all I could see was him hitting me again.

I panicked. Then I thought, I have to fight him off me one more time. To defend my daughter. Right now!

I screamed as loudly as I could: "Leave! Why don't you leave? Get out of here! Get out!"

I held my daughter tightly, as far away from him as I could. The nurse rushed in, looked at Woody and then looked at me, trying to figure out what was happening. There was more panic. More yelling. More anger and confusion.

My last thought was, How can I hold on to my baby tight enough without hurting her? Or even killing her?

I'm not quite sure what happened next. The nurse must have given me another shot, because the next thing I knew I was alone in my bed. Both my baby and Woody were gone.

Where was she? She was safe, said the nurse when I rang for her. When I begged her to show me, she brought her to my bed. They'd told my ex-husband, she said, not to come back uninvited. I never saw Woody McCorvey again.

Melissa Renee McCorvey—Missy—was a beautiful baby. She looked a lot like Woody, but that didn't matter to me at all.

Woody would have nothing to do with my child—I'd make sure of that. When we brought Melissa home to my mother's house, we put her into the crib in my bedroom. She hardly ever cried or woke me up during the night. I learned to change her, feed her, and dress her in the baby clothes my mother had bought for her at the Goodwill store.

I was as happy as I'd ever be. I went back to work after six weeks, back on the night shift at Pete's—even though, or maybe because, my mother told me it was too soon. My plan was to save up my money in the tip jar, just like before, and eventually get my own place and a babysitter for Melissa. Until then, I'd ask my mother to help raise her granddaughter.

I thought that maybe, just maybe, I could keep things calm between us. After all, in recent times we'd gotten along pretty well—and I promised her that even when we moved away, to somewhere close by, she could still be a big part of Melissa's life. But even then there were undercurrents. Bad blood from the past. Signs that I never really stopped to read.

For one thing, my mother took complete charge of Melissa the first day we got her back from the hospital. Or, at least, she tried to. She told me how to hold my daughter, how to give her her bottle, what she needed and when, and what I was doing all wrong.

All of my old resentful feelings flared up. I couldn't let her do this to me. When she criticized me I talked back to her and told her to mind her own business; sometimes I even took Missy outside to hide from her, just like when I was a little girl myself.

Things began getting worse in my mother's house—in ways I didn't really understand. One night she put an acidify ball, a Cajun herb charm, in Missy's crib. I found it the next morning. It was to chase off bad spirits, she said.

Another morning I caught her holding a pocket mirror under my daughter's mouth when she was sleeping.

"It's to check whether she's breathing," my mother told me. I thought that was very strange and scary, even for her. We needed to get away as soon as possible. But we didn't make it. In a time when I should have kept myself under the tightest control, I let my feelings run away with me.

During the months after Melissa was born I went back to my old life entirely, spending my days at home with her and my nights at Pete's. But the nights at the restaurant were just as long and lonely. Even with Missy to take care of, and my mother on my back, the walls were closing in on me.

I missed being with my friends at Sue's, especially Liz Gilliam and Glennis Long. I'd kept the number of their place in Fort Worth, and when I called them completely out of the blue they were glad to hear from me.

They invited me to visit them for the weekend. That meant asking my mother to take care of Missy for two straight days and nights. I decided to ask her. It's a measure of just how naive I was that I told her the whole truth about where I was going. And, just to clear the air, I thought it was the time to tell her the truth about myself, too.

Most afternoons, my mother took a nap in her bedroom. Occasionally, if Missy was asleep, I would lay down beside her and talk to her, exchanging neighborhood gossip, until she fell asleep.

This time I lay down beside her, not quite knowing the right way to put things. Then I thought, Well, there are no right ways or wrong ways. I blurted out that I wanted to spend the weekend in Fort Worth with Glennis Long and Liz Gilliam.

"Well, who the hell are Glennis Long and Liz Gilliam?"

I told her. I don't remember my exact words, but I tried to get across that they were two women I'd met at Sue's. Also that they were two women who loved each other and lived together, and that you could kind of say that in the months before Melissa arrived they'd sort of become my best friends.

There was a long second of silence.

"What the hell are you talking about, Norma? I've been to Sue's. My friends go there. There's nobody in there like you're talking about."

"No, Mother, you're wrong. That's the old Sue's. It's changed since we went there." Then I told her as plainly as I could what kind of women went there now.

I'd been lying on my back, looking up, but now I rolled over to face her. The expression on her face was one of pure shock. As soon as our eyes met she jumped off the bed, stood over me, and shouted, "Well, no wonder! That's why you want to come in and sleep with me in the afternoon!"

"What?" I said.

I didn't understand—not until much later—because, I think, my mother calmed down right away and said she'd be glad to take care of Melissa. Over the weekend, in Fort Worth, I had a good time with Liz and Glennis, watching TV and drinking beer and going shopping with Liz's parents.

When I got back it was the afternoon of Palm Sunday. There was a crowd of people wearing their best clothes and holding palm branches in their hands, in front of the Episcopal church across the street. When I got into the house I noticed that Mother had moved Missy's crib from my room into hers. That's all right, I thought. She was closer to help when Missy started crying. I went into her bedroom to pick up my daughter. I bent over the crib, pulled back the covers, and saw that Melissa was gone.

Instead of my baby there was a doll, a plastic-headed doll, in the crib. Was this some kind of joke? It sure didn't feel like one. My mother had heard me come in and was standing in the doorway.

"Norma, don't you want to say hello to your baby?"

"Well, Mom," I said, "that's where I am right now."

"Don't you think she looks a lot better?" she said.

"What the hell do you mean? What's this doll doing in here?"

"Well, that's your baby, Norma," she said, with a funny expression on her face. "We were hoping that you wouldn't notice."

Those were her exact words. I remember them too well. And even though I didn't really understand why at the time, they sent a flash of fear right through me. But I fought that first fear down.

"Mother, where's Melissa?" I said as calmly as I possibly could.

"Well, you don't need to know that," she said. "All you need to know is that you have to get out. I've turned you in for abandonment."

It still made no sense.

"You've turned me in for what?"

"Well, you went off and abandoned your baby."

"What?"

No. It was too awful even to think about. The fear began to change to panic, edged with anger.

"What the hell is going on?"

"Well, you've been gone all weekend, Norma, and I guess you didn't think that this child had to eat, and had to be fed, and had to be cleaned."

The awful possibility began to take shape in mind. Had my mother taken Melissa? Had she had actually stolen my baby?

A crazy thought: Maybe because her own daughter had turned out so badly, and she couldn't have any more babies of her own, she had kidnapped mine.

"What are you talking about? Didn't I tell you where I was going? Didn't I tell you when I was coming back?"

She shook her head.

"Where is my baby?" I said angrily. "What the hell have you done with my baby?"

"You don't have to know that, Norma," said my mother.

Then her mouth was moving and terrible words were coming out. She was telling me that I'd abandoned Melissa. Given her up to her. So she would step in and raise her granddaughter by herself. Take care of her, all by herself. Melissa was hers.

I tried to think of what I should do, what any mother would do, but before I could do anything at all the surprise wore off and anger rose up inside me. It was the same anger I had felt when Woody had hit me, only bigger, bigger than ever, and I could not choke it down.

I became full of my anger, on fire with my anger. All the rage I had ever known came back at that one moment and took hold of me. I could have killed my mother, or anyone, but I was too angry even for that.

And then, to my everlasting sorrow, I lost everything. At the most important moment in my life, when the daughter I loved needed me to be calm and smart and under control, I gave in to my anger.

I became my anger. And I lost my daughter. My only daughter. And the worst part—the absolute worst part—was that somewhere, even at that moment of insanity, I knew that I was failing her.

I screamed at my mother, as loud and as long as I could,

"What are you doing? What are you doing? Where's Melissa? Where is she? What are you doing? What are you doing?"

"Calm down," she said. "She's all right. But I'll take care of her now."

"Where is she? Give her back to me! Where is she?" My mother stood still with her arms folded. I raced around the house, looking in closets and in the other beds, for Melissa. She wasn't there. I screamed and cried for her, still cursing my mother and Raymond.

Then there was a knock at the door, and my father, whom I hadn't seen for a long time, came in. Behind him were two Dallas policemen. All right! They would certainly see the crime that was going on here.

One of them walked up to me. "You're making a disturbance, girl," he said. "There's been a complaint. We're going to have ask you to leave."

"Fine," I said, struggling as hard as I could to calm down. "Great! I'm going to leave. I wouldn't stay in this fucking house another minute. But I won't leave without my baby."

"What baby?" he said.

My mother shook her head again.

"My baby!" I shouted.

I grabbed his arm and pulled him over to the crib.

"Look at this! They've stolen my baby! They've stolen my baby! They've stolen my baby and left this doll in her place! I want you to arrest this woman for kidnapping my daughter!"

I looked across the room at my father. He looked sad, not mad. He wasn't there to help me. He was on the other side.

"Isn't this pitiful?" said my mother to the policeman.

"Listen, Miss," said the cop, "I'm not leaving here till you do."

I thought: He doesn't believe me! He thinks I'm talking about an imaginary baby!

"Miss, if you continue making a disturbance right here we're gonna have to take you downtown with us."

And then something sane and calm deep down inside me—or was it really just the anger in disguise?—told me to leave now, before I did something even worse than what I was doing at the moment. Before I got even deeper in trouble. Even further from ever getting Melissa back.

"All right. I'm leaving right now."

I called Sue's. Liz was already there. I screamed into the phone at her, trying to explain, somehow, what was going on.

"Are the cops there?" she asked. When I said yes, she told me to shut the hell up and leave the apartment. Then she got in her car and picked me up on the street corner outside.

~ 8 ~

It was 1967 when the pregnant Sarah Weddington, still a law student, decided that having a baby would seriously threaten her dream of becoming a lawyer. At that time abortion was illegal in Texas, but luckily for her—and for the pro-choice movement—she was able to get an abortion anyway.

Sarah writes about this abortion in her autogiography. Her husband, Ron Weddington, asked around among their college friends in Austin and got the name of an abortion clinic across the border in Mexico. Abortions were illegal in Mexico, too, but if you had the money and knew the right place to go to the chances of being arrested were pretty small.

It's easy for me to imagine how terrifying it must have been for a woman like Sarah to travel to a dusty little town in a foreign country and trust her body to strangers. Fortunately, she had her husband along to help her. The abortion clinic turned out to be a safe one, and for $400—which would be a few thousand dollars today—she was able to terminate her pregnancy and get back to her studies.

Sarah graduated from law school with high marks, but because of the widespread discrimination against women in the legal world she couldn't get a job in a regular law firm. This gave her an added reason to fight for women's causes. She went to work for one of her law professors, helping to rewrite the lawyers' rules of ethics for the American Bar Association.

In her spare time she went to women's consciousness-raising groups and helped out on a local underground newspaper that was beginning to editorialize for legalized abortion. The newspaper also ran articles listing safe birth control methods and warnings against unsafe or ineffective self-abortion procedures.

Sarah met and became close to a group of women who ran a hotline for birth control and abortion information. Secretly, this group also referred women to illegal—but relatively safe—abortion clinics and doctors in the United States and Mexico. Sarah writes that she herself never volunteered any of this information to pregnant women, but she did advise the members of the secret abortion-referral group on the legal risks they were running—and the penalties and sentences they would face—if they were ever caught.

Gradually this work turned into an exploration of whether the Texas anti-abortion law could be overturned. This got Sarah started on a long legal research project on the subject, and she gained a lot of knowledge of the history of abortion laws in America.

She was especially interested in *Griswold* v. *Connecticut,* a case that had only recently overturned a state ban against selling birth control devices. She began to think that a similar case could overturn the anti-abortion laws. She also realized that starting and running such a case would be a long and complicated job—one better suited to a group of high-powered, well-paid lawyers with a big staff to support them. These kinds of lawyers, however, were not likely to take on such a case for free.

For a young, inexperienced lawyer like Sarah, the odds were horribly against her. But Sarah Weddington won her place in history by deciding to take the case anyway. She went to work for no money, with the help of her husband and good friends and law school classmates like Linda Coffee. Sarah used her incredible energy and concentration to make up for her lack of experience.

Eventually, after gathering all her information and tapping the knowledge of many of her teachers at Austin, she decided that the best way to overturn the anti-abortion law was to find women affected by the law and challenge it in court. These women would be her plaintiffs in the case.

The first woman Sarah found was a college professor who had a health condition that would make it dangerous for her to become pregnant. The same condition also prevented her from taking birth control pills. In Sarah's lawsuit, this plaintiff remained anonymous under the name of "Mary Doe."

Then, Sarah and her legal team decided that using only Mary Doe as a plaintiff was not enough. They also needed a woman who was actually pregnant—and who couldn't get an abortion but still didn't want to bear her child.

That kind of woman was harder to find.

9

The world is often very confusing to me, and the rules seem to shift with whoever is following them, but of one thing I am absolutely certain: leaving Melissa with my mother was the worst thing I have ever done. If I had swallowed my pride and kept my temper, I could have fought off my mother somehow and taken my little girl away with me.

Melissa was my daughter, my firstborn, and I was ready to do what I had to do to take care of her. Whatever the situation I was in, wherever my past and present had taken me, I should not have abandoned her.

It's no use for anyone, friend or otherwise, to tell me differently. However they try to help me remember, I cannot tell myself that I gave up Melissa for her own good.

To some people, an eighteen-year-old lesbian waitress might not have seemed like a good mother for a baby. But these people never knew the love I had, and still have, for Melissa. In my mind and in my heart, I know I would have been a good mother to her. And our lives—both of our lives—would have turned out completely differently.

It was a possibility worth dying for. But I didn't. Not then, anyway. Instead, I failed my daughter. At the moment she needed me I failed her totally. I've lived to blame myself for my failure ever since. And I will take that sorrow to my grave.

I got drunk that night at Sue's, and I stayed at Liz and Glennis's place for the next week. I called my mother every day, screaming and pleading with her, but she wouldn't tell me where my baby was.

She just said that Melissa was all right where she was. Every day after that was the same. I was so full of rage and guilt and fear that I could barely dial the phone. Only when I drank—and I needed to drink three or four beers to begin to drown my feelings—could I force myself to begin thinking halfway normally. When I could think normally, in the little space before I was completely drunk, I realized I would have to calm down considerably before I could try to fight my mother.

I quit my job at Pete's and started work as a waitress at the White Carriage, a predominantly male gay bar. I rented my own apartment. I held off calling my mother until I was absolutely in control of myself, and I managed to talk to her calmly longer and longer each time.

"We're only doing this because it's best for Melissa," she'd say. After a few weeks I could even listen to her say this to me without slamming down the phone. After a couple of months she let me visit Melissa, who was back at her house. But she never let the baby out of her sight. She said she was in contact with the county child welfare people about me, and if I tried to take her back, she'd get total legal control of Melissa. She also talked and talked to me about Raymond's health insurance policy. How she was trying to get Melissa included in it. How if anything happened to Raymond—if he lost a finger, or an arm, or a leg—then the company would pay Melissa a certain amount of money for each.

She decided that she would let me move back in—as her daughter, not Melissa's mother. I felt that this might be my first step toward getting Melissa back. I was as wrong as I'd ever been.

One night I came in after my shift at the White Carriage and some heavy drinking I'd done afterwards, at about four in the morning. My mother woke me up at eight.

The woman from the insurance company was there, she said, and she was waiting for me to sign the papers needed to put Melissa on Raymond's policy.

I told her I was too tired, that I could do it another time, but she wouldn't let me go back to sleep. She reminded me that I was a guest in her house. I knew what that meant. I went into the front room, shook hands with the woman, and signed next to all the X's on the papers she had brought with her.

I crawled back into bed and tried to get back to sleep. I heard her show the woman out and the front door close behind her. Five minutes later she opened the hall closet, pulled out my suitcase, and threw it on the bed next to me.

"You've got exactly five minutes to pack all your shit and get out of our lives," she said.

"What?" I said, half awake.

"I've just adopted your daughter from underneath you. You stupid goddamn little ignorant! I just took your child away from you legally!"

Then she began to stomp through the house, cursing me and calling me a queer and a pervert and a lowlife who would never amount to anything good.

I got up and walked into the kitchen and made myself a cup of coffee. Then, horribly, it began to sink in what she had done to me. No, God help me—what I had done to myself!

I panicked, then went beyond panic to despair. Black despair. I had been so stupid, so careless, such a bad mother, that I had signed away my baby. And there was nothing I could now. Nothing I could think of. There was no way out. Not in this lifetime, anyway.

Every bit of self-respect I still had disappeared. Every bit of anything that was good about me, every reason that I deserved to be Melissa's mother—I could feel them all melting away.

All that was left was the anger, bubbling underneath. That was the only thing keeping me going. It was the only thing keeping me alive.

Trembling, I got dressed, packed up my things, and got ready to go.

My mother flung open the front door and cursed me again. I grabbed her by the throat and pushed her against the wall. I told her that if I ever saw her again, after this morning, I would kill her. And then all I could trust myself to do was pull myself away from her and leave her house forever.

My mother and Raymond took over raising Melissa. They moved from place to place a lot, around Dallas and other parts of

Texas and once even back to Louisiana. They rarely told me when
or where they were moving. I tried to keep track of their movements, and when I knew where my daughter was, and thought I
could keep control of myself, I called my mother to ask if I could
visit Melissa. Sometimes she would be in a good mood toward me,
and sometimes her mood was very bad.

The hardest parts came when she turned me down. Not much
better were the times she did let me see Melissa, and I had to head
back to my house empty-handed.

I was so alone that I became part of another family, a much bigger one that didn't judge me nearly as harshly as my real one did.

The Dallas gay bar scene was absolutely thriving back then,
although if you would have asked a straight person about it, he or
she would have looked at you like you were crazy. Or maybe they
would have called the police. Or knocked you down right there in
the street.

The truth was, nobody talked to straight people about such
things. That would only bring trouble. And we knew this, too: if we
drank and partied in the right bars and made sure that most of the
people we knew were the ones we met there, it could almost seem
like the straight world outside, with all the troubles it held for us,
didn't exist.

The bars sponsored softball leagues and pool tournaments,
dances, road trips, and Sunday picnics. It also helped that there was
always an opening for a good bartender. And that was me. I might
not have had much of an education, but I made a great little teenage
bartender. I was friendly when I could be, tough when I had to be. I
knew everybody's name, and everybody's drink, and I would gladly
talk to any of my customers if they wanted conversation.

Best of all, when my shift was over I'd go around to the other
side of the bar, order three or four beers, and smoke cigarettes and
whoop and holler as loudly as the rest of them. I'd rarely go home
before closing time, and whether I'd gone home alone or not, I'd
be back to open up the place by ten or eleven the next morning. I
did my best to stay out of the daylight.

I moved from the White Carriage to the Red Devil, a women's
bar. I made a fresh set of friends, which was easy to do in those
days. I got my nickname, Pixie, because I was so small and I moved
so quickly.

My first real grownup love affair was with a regular customer, Carol Borders.* I met her the same day she graduated from charm school—she walked into the bar that Friday afternoon and it was love at first sight. Carol lived with her parents in the rich part of Dallas, in a house so big that it scared me when we drove past it.

Carol was beautiful and smart, and she took pains always to dress in a ladylike manner, with perfect makeup and perfect hair—perfectly teased and curled and frosted. She was a computer operator—actually, a "data processor," which is what they called women who did computer work—and she told me she had enrolled in charm school because she couldn't figure out why she didn't have a boyfriend.

Only when she was drunk could she be halfway comfortable as my girlfriend. But it was no good even then—when we were both drunk, she would catch me flirting with other customers, and we would have loud fights and arguments, both of us yelling and screaming, which were definitely not ladylike.

Susan Sanderson* was the opposite of Carol. No nonsense, straightforward, uncomplicated. Blue collar. She worked over at Baylor University Hospital as a respiratory therapist. She came into the bar nearly every night. She knew she was a lesbian—no ifs, ands, or buts—and when we fell in love with each other she had no trouble at all deciding to move in with me. We rented a place near the hospital and set up house.

Then the Red Devil changed ownership, as all the bars did after awhile. With a new manager, it wasn't half as good either drinking or working there.

"What kind of education did you have?" Susan asked me one day. I told her the truth, and the amazing thing was that even when I did, she was able to get me a job interview at the hospital. They never asked me if I'd graduated from high school—just my birth date and when I could start work. After a three-day orientation course, most of it spent learning how to work and take care of a an oxygen machine, I was a respiratory therapist, too. I was all set to take the graveyard shift at Baylor.

I did just what they told me. I wore a white uniform, white hose, and white shoes. I had my name tag that said: NORMA, RESPIRATORY THERAPIST. I worked from 11 P.M. to 7 A.M. Two full weeks on and one week off. Every night, I took apart and cleaned all the oxygen machines—the Intermittent Positive Pressure Breathing Apparatuses—that weren't then in use.

I also administered oxygen to the patients. During the first few months I was terrified I would make a mistake and kill somebody. But I never did. Maybe that was the patients' good luck, or mine, or both. I saw enough people die, from cancer, mostly—many of them "my" patients, everyone from nine-year-old children to 101-year-old great-grandmothers. I saw housewives in their forties and fifties, after their hysterectomies, lying in bed and wondering out loud if they were still women, if their lives were over. I saw huge men, tough-looking Texans wearing ten-gallon hats and gleaming white cowboy shirts, on their knees in the corridors, sobbing. Their wives, or their children, or their parents were dying, and all their strength and hope was just melting away.

And I listened to the loudspeaker, because at least once a shift there was a page for Dr. Hart.

There was no Dr. Hart. When we heard "Paging Dr. Hart" over the loudspeakers, it meant that a patient—somewhere—was having trouble breathing. Or had stopped breathing. I listened to hear which room they were sending Dr. Hart to, and then I would rush there with the apparatus. Sometimes the patients' lungs would be filling up with fluid. Sometimes they would be suffering heart attacks, or choking on their ventilator or on their own vomit. Sometimes they would already be dying in front of my eyes.

Many of the graveyard staffers drank on the job. Art,* our shift boss, liked to bring a bottle of vodka and a watermelon to work. After we'd finish our eleven o'clock appointments he'd drill holes in the watermelon, pour vodka into the holes, put the plugs back in, and haul it downstairs to an empty slab in the morgue to cool. A few hours later he'd bring the watermelon back up to our department on the fourth floor. We'd eat our lunch and dessert together. One night, when all the slabs were full, Art moved a corpse out into the hallway to make room.

Nobody ever caught us. By three or four in the morning most of the doctors and many of the nurses had gone home, and just about the only sound we heard was the coughing of the patients who couldn't sleep. Or were too afraid to sleep. That was what some of the bravest ones told me.

The work was scary, nerve-racking—and boring, all at the same time. But the good part was that I was earning much more than I ever had. There were some unheard-of added extras, such as health insurance and paid holidays and social security, thrown in. I joined the hospital credit union and began saving a good part of my paycheck each week. It made me feel very adult and responsible.

I still raised hell in the bars on my evenings off. The problem was that Susan's week off rarely came at the same time as mine, and sometimes when we were off together, she would drive to Houston to visit her parents. That made me lonely and envious at the same time. And once we saved up a little bit of money together, we began to have arguments about how we were going to spend it. Susan's car payments? Some new clothes from the Spiegel catalog? Next month's rent? Also, a man who worked at the hospital was bothering me. Actually, bothering me was too strong a word for it.

The first time Pete Hidalgo* spoke to me, I was standing in an alcove, waiting for the elevator. It was one, maybe two o'clock in the morning.

"Oh, boy. You sure smell good!" said a male voice behind me.

I turned around angrily. I saw a short, dark-haired Hispanic man in a white uniform. He was smiling, but not a mean smile.

"*Excuse* me?"

"Yes. You sure do smell good. What kind of perfume are you wearing?"

No man had ever asked me that. I told him as roughly as I could that I owned two kinds of perfume, but that I didn't remember which one I was wearing. I thought that would make him shut up or go away, but for some reason he didn't. He told me his name was Pete, that he was from New Mexico, but he had graduated from college right here in Texas. Now he was working as an orderly to get money for medical school. I told him that was great, and when the elevator door opened, I got in and rode up to my floor alone.

*   *   *

I didn't give Pete a second thought—except maybe that he'd sure picked the wrong girl to hit on. But in the next few weeks I began to hear some strange things: that Pete had talked to Art and gotten my schedule. That he'd changed his own schedule to match mine. That he wanted to ask me out. I began to bump into Pete in the hallways. He was always nice, always soft-spoken. He asked me out to lunch in the hospital cafeteria. What was the harm?

At lunch he told was going to be become a doctor and then go back to work in his home state. He asked me to go out with him outside the hospital, and I turned him down. Susan and I were having bigger troubles than ever, but this wasn't the answer. But as usual, that didn't stop me from making the absolute worst out of the situation.

Early one morning, walking home from work to an empty apartment, I heard fast footsteps behind me. I was scared. I whirled around. It was Pete.

"Aren't you cold?" he said.

He was right. I was shivering. Then he took off his jacket and put it around my shoulders.

He asked me to let him buy me a hamburger, and we went to an all-night place nearby. He talked about books he'd read and art films he'd seen and his plans for helping "his people" back in New Mexico when he became a doctor. As he talked, I studied his face closely. There was something soft, almost feminine about Pete Hidalgo. Despite Susan, despite Woody, despite everything, I felt confusing stirrings of feelings inside.

The next night I cornered him in the hospital corridor and came right out with it: I told him that I was living with a woman, that I slept with this woman, and asked him what he could figure out from my telling him that. He took my hand and told me it didn't matter to him at all.

My week off began a few days later. Susan, as usual, was out of town. I spent those seven days with Pete, most of it in my apartment. After he made love to me I douched, although in the back of my mind I knew that it wouldn't keep me from getting in trouble. Even further back, I suppose, I was certain I would.

When we left the house we went to straight bars and restaurants. Pete didn't drink much. He just liked to listen to me talk. I think he saw me as a kind of dangerous person. To him I was exciting, adventurous—as if my life had been some kind of thrill ride I'd chosen to take.

By the end of the week, the excitement had worn off for both of us. I told him that it had been nice, in some ways, but there was really no future for us. I said I was sorry that I hadn't told him at the beginning, because there were still some doubts in the back of my mind, but the fact was I wasn't meant to stay with any man. Pete was disappointed, but he didn't seem to take it too badly. When I went back to work, I hardly ran into him in the hospital at all.

Susan finally came back to town and of course heard from her friends at the hospital everything she needed to hear about Pete and me. We broke up for good after a couple of knockdown, drag-out fights. It was right after I moved out and got my own apartment that I started to feel the now familiar signs of pregnancy.

This time, I didn't feel scared or nervous—at least on the surface. On the surface, I was disgusted with my stupid and worthless self. I wasn't even a good enough mother to keep my firstborn daughter with me. I thought, What business do you, Norma McCorvey, have bearing another baby? Norma McCorvey was trash. She was the lowest of the low.

Underneath the surface, I could feel a hot river of pain and hopelessness churning up—maybe a lot more of it than even I could imagine, much less deal with. So I pushed it all down and closed the lid.

I called Pete and told him the news. He came over, and like the gentleman he was, offered to marry me. I thanked him, but told him that living as a housewife in a little house with a white picket fence around it was just not how I saw my life going. Not anymore.

"But what about our baby?" he said.

I told him that I'd thought that all out, also. Before the baby was born, I would sign it away for adoption. I would tell him when I was going into the hospital. If he wanted to take the baby for his own, he could deal with the authorities before then. If not, that was fine, too. Hopefully the baby would find a good family.

Pete thanked me and left. I never saw him again. A few days

afterwards I told Grace, the hospital supervisor, what my situation was. She fired me on the spot. There was a rule, she told me, against female employees becoming pregnant out of wedlock. Even then, it sounded unfair, old-fashioned, and illegal. But "out of wedlock" was exactly how she said it.

When I was pregnant with my second child I was alone, living off my credit union savings and waiting for the time to pass so I could get on with my life. Deliberately, I tried not to get too involved with the baby inside me, because then I would want to keep her—and that would be selfish, and wrong, because she would never be able to get the chance in life she deserved.

I spent the days and months inside my apartment, thinking of all the mistakes I'd made and kicking myself for always managing to make new ones. I wondered over and over: what was the secret to a decent, sometimes halfway happy life? What part of the goddamn puzzle had I not been given?

But although I thought and thought, the answer would just not come to me. In the evenings, when I found myself sitting alone in the dark, I'd leave the apartment and walk to the only place I knew where people could leave me alone in my misery and be near me, all at the same time. Then I drank to make the misery go away.

I don't know what happened to my second baby, who her parents are. I've never laid eyes on her. Since I'd given her up for adoption, the people at Dallas Osteopathic never brought her into my room. When I woke up, they told me she had already gone home with her new family. One of the doctors let it slip that I'd had a boy. A nurse told me otherwise, that I'd had a girl. Another nurse said that a Spanish man, who came with an older woman who looked a lot like him—his mother?—had picked her out when I was still unconscious. Those are the hard, cold facts of it, for which I am totally responsible.

One thing worries me the most. They say that when a woman is pregnant, how she feels and acts can influence her unborn baby in all sorts of long lasting, maybe even permanent ways. I hope in my guilty heart that things have worked out otherwise.

A few weeks out of the hospital, I went back to the only world where I thought—no, where I was absolutely certain—I belonged.

Anyplace where I might run into Susan or her friends was off-limits. So during the day I tended bar at the Roadrunner, a place in East Dallas that attracted both lesbians and straight men. It was owned by a man named James, who was middle-aged and talked like a character in a gangster movie. At night I walked across the street to work at the Sultan's Harem, a straight place that James owned, too.

Both the Roadrunner and the Sultan's Harem had go-go dancers. At the Roadrunner, the dancers wore minidresses. At the Sultan's Harem, they wore gauzy Arabian costumes.

These weren't cozy neighborhood taverns. The real point of both places was for the girls to take breaks from dancing, sit in the customers' laps, and make them buy expensive glasses—or if they were really drunk, whole bottles—of cheap champagne.

I wasn't one of the girls. I wore black polyester pants and white Ship 'n Shore blouses. My job was to keep an eye on the go-go dancers, to make sure they were spending enough time with each customer, and to see that there were always full cases of pink bubbly bathwater lined up behind the bar.

I hired and fired the dancers, also. At the Roadrunner and Sultan's Harem, the dancing requirements weren't too high. You just had to bounce up and down and look like you were enjoying yourself. One Friday evening a beautiful, thin brunette named Renee* came into the Harem looking for a job.

I gave Renee some coins to play three songs on the jukebox. Renee really could dance. More important, by the second song I was madly in love with her.

Renee wasn't a lesbian, but she turned out to be an important person in my life anyway. I hired her and gave her three of the best shifts—Thursday, Friday, and Saturday nights. I decided I would definitely keep my eye on her. We became friendly right away.

"How do you get the energy to do both jobs?" she asked me. "It's tough," I said. At that point I was working fifteen hours a day, seven days a week.

Renee took a couple of pills out of her back pocket. "Well, Norma, when you're feeling a little sleepy, try these."

I tried them on a Saturday night. By the time I got back to the Roadrunner on Monday morning I had pulled a couple of double shifts, gone home, cleaned and dusted my house, completely rearranged my furniture, washed and perfectly ironed all my clothes, and stayed up the rest of the night watching old television shows. On Monday I called a general meeting of all the girls from both bars and lectured them for an hour about the need to keep the champagne moving. How James was counting on us, how we all had to pull together and make sure that half-empty cases didn't keep piling up. They looked at me as if I was crazy. I felt as if my eyelashes were glued open. By Wednesday I had still not gone to sleep, my house was cleaner than ever, and I was more tired than I had ever been.

I collapsed and slept for fourteen hours.

When I woke up I went to the bar, looked up Renee's address on her job application, and took a cab over to her place for a visit.

Renee lived on Rolling Rock Street, in a big but run-down house. When she opened the front door she was dressed differently than I'd ever seen her, in an Indian peasant shirt, bell-bottom jeans, sandals, and a headband.

"Hi, Norma!" she said, glad to see me.

When I asked her what was in the pills she'd given me, she seemed surprised that I hadn't known.

"They're diet pills," she told me. "Black Mollies. They work great, don't they?"

She introduced me to her roommates. They were all hippies, the first I'd come across in Dallas. Just like the ones from California I'd seen in the newspapers. Wind was a boy and Rain was a girl. Bubba was Renee's brother. He showed me his secret plan, all drawn out on notebook paper, to blow up the big electricity generating plant at White Rock Lake. He asked me if I would help him do it when the time was exactly right. I told him I was sorry, that it just wasn't my cup of tea.

Renee invited me to stay for dinner: we ate what she called Hippie Soup, made with chicken bouillon, egg noodles, and every spice and condiment on the kitchen shelf. It didn't taste bad at all. Renee's roommates all seemed to be nice people, people who liked me even though I was different from them. When I got up to leave, they made me sit back down on the pillows on the floor and talk with them. I decided to stay over—and didn't leave until it was way beyond late.

* * *

By the time I met Renee, I'd already heard a lot about LSD. From what people were saying at the bar—and at the bar, of course, everybody knew exactly what they were talking about—it sounded like this new drug could free your mind from the distractions and complications of the real world. Once that happened, you could come up with answers to questions you'd been worrying about for a long time. Although it sounded like bullshit, finding answers was certainly something that I would like to do. Maybe I could even find Melissa.

"Have you ever tripped?" Renee asked me one day.

Underneath her hippie clothes—sometimes she even painted a big yellow sun on her cheek—Renee was really just an old-fashioned drug dealer. Besides hash and pot and speed, Renee specialized in acid.

"No," I said.

"Well then, Norma, it's time."

Renee handed me a piece of construction paper and told me to bite down and chew on it.

"I can't eat paper. It makes me constipated," I said.

Renee laughed. She said that was the funniest thing she'd heard in a long time. As I stuck the construction paper into my mouth, she said she loved the way I looked at life.

Life looked pretty much the same for the next half-hour. Then I noticed that the living room wall was melting, from the ceiling down. I figured I should go get a broom and dustpan to sweep it back up.

I wandered outside the house to find the broom, but first I saw a big staircase, up against the side of the house, that hadn't been there before. The individual stair steps all folded one way, then the other way, and then, incredibly, the whole staircase began moving toward me.

When I walked out of its way it disappeared. When I turned my head to look for it again, my eye was drawn to a tree in the backyard. It was ugly and bare, because it was February. But as I stared, leaves began to grow on the tree's bare branches. Then there were apples all over it, and birds singing, and the next thing I knew I was sitting inside the house again, shivering.

Renee and Wind and Rain were sitting next to me, smiling. They told me that I'd been standing outside the house for hours, just staring at the tree.

"How did you like your first acid trip?" Renee asked me.

Well, there weren't any answers, I thought. But maybe I just didn't ask the right questions.

The next part of the story will sound familiar, and sadly so, to anyone old enough to have lived through that time.

I spent a lot of time at Renee's crash pad, dropping acid and talking about peace and love and revolution and hanging out with fellow enlightened people in the park by Lake Dallas. Bubba never did blow up the power station. He died the next year from an overdose of Dilantin, which is synthetic heroin.

As for me, the drugs never did help me find the answers. But they did what seemed to be the next best thing: they kept most of the questions away. And most of the world away. At least for a while.

I completely changed the way I dressed. I threw out my work clothes and bought jeans and midriff tops and bandanna headbands. Instead of pulling all the bar shifts I could, I started showing up late and then missing work altogether. I tripped during work, too. The balls on the pool table stretched out and squashed themselves flat. They crawled, not rolled, across the table. James fired me, for damn good cause.

Renee told me not to worry, that I could work for her. She started me off by giving me two hundred hits of her acid to sell. I let it be known around the neighborhood that I was open for business. Each hit was three dollars—two for Renee and one for me. Throughout the day, usually every half-hour, someone would knock on my window and I would make a sale.

As a bonus, in the spirit of our friendship, Renee gave me a list of doctors who would write just about anyone a prescription for diet pills. I traveled around Dallas being physically examined by these men. I was bone thin, but that was no problem. After the doctors examined me they always agreed that I could stand to lose a little more weight. The standard "scrip" they wrote for me, nonrenewable until after another visit, was for thirty Black Mollies. I sold this drug for three dollars per unit also, and it was pure profit, no money back to Renee, less the price of my "exams." I held back five out of every thirty pills. Those I kept for my personal use.

Most of my customers were male strangers, although I had a regular clientele of prostitutes—working girls like Zyla and Donna, who stopped off for a pick-me-up on the way to a "date" at the apparel mart, or wherever. Although none of them were what even I would call glamorous, I was always glad to see them. They didn't always have time to talk, or answer my naive questions about their working life, but they never gave me any trouble or backtalk.

I was never arrested. No policemen ever even came around. That didn't mean that I wasn't worried about being caught. When I didn't have to be there, I spent as little time in the apartment as possible. At the time I thought it was just common sense. Now I realize that it was common sense plus a lot of pure extra-strength speed.

An odd thing about this time period—much of which I've forgotten, a lot more of which I'd like to—was that I decided, after going years without seeing him, to find my father. It was surprisingly easy. As an extremely free person I had all the time in the world to find him. I asked at a few TV repair shops around town for Jimmy Nelson, and in a day or two I was at the door of his apartment, face to face with him.

"Can I help you?" he said.

"Dad, it's Norma," I said.

He took a closer look at the hippie girl standing in front of him.

"Hi, Norma!" He said it just like it had been a week or two since we'd last seen each other.

My dad was as gentle and forgetful as ever. He still spent most of his time with his tubes and transistors, losing himself. He lived in a duplex owned by May, his girlfriend. When I met May, a nice, gentle middle-aged woman, she said there was an empty apartment I could move right into, if I could pay some rent. I could.

I had a lot of restlessness and paranoia to work off. Crazily, I needed to be around other people as much as I needed to be alone. After Bubba died, Wind and Rain split for California and Renee was too involved in her drug-dealing problems to spend much time with me. That probably saved my life.

I began to go back to the White Carriage, this time as a customer.

By the late sixties the Carriage was pretty much a lesbian bar, with a sprinkling of straight male regulars who liked to play pool with the women. To work off my extra energy I played pool with the men—and cut back on the acid trips so that the cue balls stayed round. At that time in my life, doing such a thing seemed to me to be the absolute height of brilliant good sense and long-range planning.

After all, I knew I was a great pool player. I shot a pretty mean stick. Ol' Pixie had a one-handed stroke and her own beautiful twenty-one-ounce custom screw-together pool cue. I organized tournaments and held the bets and divided up the prize money.

I knew everyone. Everyone knew me. Except maybe the strange-looking man who came into the bar one Saturday night. I'd never seen him before.

He looked about fifty, but he was still long and lean. He had a scar across his mouth and a finger missing from his right hand. Unlike all the lunchpail cowboys who played at the Carriage, he wore gray knit slacks and a formal-looking white shirt. When he came in the door, he walked straight toward me.

"The answer is yes," I told him. "I'll be your partner."

"How did you know I was going to ask you?" he said.

"Because I'm the last one without a partner, and so are you, and that kinda gives me the idea of what's going to happen here. Yes, I'll be your partner, and yes, I'll play for five dollars a ball, and yes, I can rack myself up."

The man laughed. And then he told his name was Carl.* When we started to play together I could see that he was an excellent player, much better even than me, playing just good enough to win all our matches. By the end of the evening we'd won the tournament, a few side bets, and had $100 in our pockets.

For some reason, after it was all over I told him something that I hadn't yet told anyone:

"You know, I really feel I have to get away from Dallas."

"I know you do," grinned Carl. "So do I."

* * *

Carl told me that he was a professional gambler. Eventually, this is what else I learned about him: that in the past ten years or so, he'd spent a lot of time gambling in Las Vegas. That he drove a big two-year-old Oldsmobile, and drank whiskey sours. Lots of them. That he drank while he was shooting pool, and eventually he got very drunk, but never until after our last game was over. That he had a girlfriend named Anne, who was brunette and slim and about thirty-five.

Anne told me that Carl came from a large poor family, but that he'd managed to work his way to a scholarship and get a college education. He could have easily become a businessman or a politician, she said, if he hadn't become fascinated with the odds and the excitement and decided that gambling was his life's work.

Carl worked hard at gambling, as hard as anybody with a regular job. He'd gamble on anything: on when the sun was going to come up, on the next day's weather, on the number of cases of beer behind the bar. Usually, because he'd worked hard at knowing the answer ahead of time, he won his bets.

Carl had been married: he had a bunch of ex-wives and children and even grandchildren, somewhere. He had a deep, strong, voice, like a radio announcer's, and he had all sorts of inside knowledge opinions about history and politics and what was going on in the world. I could listen to him for hours. Just about anyone who knew him could.

Carl lived in a big rented house in the hills and had the biggest, most expensive-looking stereo I'd ever seen. The most expensive part was a big, top-of-the-line, reel-to-reel tape recorder. Like the ones they had in recording studios, he said. With it, he never had to listen to one record at a time, like most people. He'd spent years recording his own special tapes—ten or twelve hours long, filled with jazz, blues, Wes Montgomery, Chopin—and he played those instead.

He threw lots of big parties in that house. I was invited to them, although I never felt all that comfortable. The guests at Carl's parties, where he played his tapes and played a pretty mean piano himself, were lots of people who looked and dressed like himself and Anne.

I never did find out how he had gotten his scar or lost his finger.

*   *   *

After that first night at the Carriage, Carl asked me to be his partner at other tournaments, at other bars around Dallas. There was something mysterious, dangerous, intriguing about him. Even to me. There was a buzz about Carl—a feeling, a confidence, a sense that there were shortcuts to wealth, maybe even happiness, that only he knew about. And the money I'd made playing with him was more than I'd made in a week of dealing. I said yes without even a second thought.

I was Carl's steady partner for about six months. Anne would come with us to the tournaments, watching us at the bar while we played. Most of the places we played were straight bars, and I was the only woman player. We'd win one, two, three matches—and then we were gone. Carl never let us play in the same place too often. He never criticized me when I missed a shot, even if it cost us money.

After a full circuit around Dallas, we wound up back at the Carriage. That was the night that Anne pulled me aside and asked me if I normally hung out with the kind of women who were at the bar. I told her I did. She asked me if I liked to have sex with women. I told her yes.

Instead of being turned off or disgusted by that, she was curious. And, in a strange way, excited. She said that she'd been thinking about those kinds of feelings in herself—and would I like to form a threesome with Carl and her?

I just stared at her. Anne told me she and Carl were "swingers." That meant there were no pledges between them, no promises, no tired old rules. Everybody slept with who they wanted to, no regrets. The people they partied with were swingers, too.

I told her thanks, but no thanks. Told her I liked her all right, but that I didn't swing with anybody.

On our last bar-crawl together, Anne came up to me and said, "Norma, I had this mysterious dream about you and Carl sleeping together."

It wasn't just a dream, I told her. It had happened. Carl and I had been sleeping together for four weeks.

If she had asked me why, which she didn't, I wouldn't have been able to tell her, exactly. Except that Carl was the closest person in the world to me then. If I'd had the time or courage to think about it, I would have probably realized that what he really was was a fellow damned soul in his own living hell.

In my half-drugged mind, though, I told myself that Carl was the perfect lover for me: no lies, no ties, no bullshit about true love or commitments.

I knew it wouldn't last. That Carl would hit the road and I would be back on my own, shifting for myself again. But until then, we were rebels, outlaws together, and that he truly understood my soul.

The night we first slept together, just when I was feeling my loneliest, he leaned down and whispered in my ear: "I think you know how I feel about you."

Anne disappeared the night she learned that Carl was cheating on her with me. I spent the next week shacked up in Carl's big house, with him and his liquor and his music. And a few pills, of course.

After a few days we both got restless, each in our own way. I felt a huge pang of guilt about Melissa, combined with more than a little bit of drug dealer paranoia. Carl felt the pull of the gambling tables, of "action." He wanted us to drive, just the two of us, all the way to Las Vegas.

I asked him if he could drive out of his way to Louisiana, where my mother was living with Melissa.

"Sure, honey," said Carl.

I put all the things I needed in a knapsack. We piled into Carl's car and he drove us straight though to Simmesport.

We talked about a lot of things on that drive, and we listened to a lot of music on the radio, but somehow we never got around to discussing whether he would wait for me. At the end of our long ride he drove up to my mother's trailer, dropped me off, waved, and drove straight onto the road out of town.

I wasn't surprised. We hadn't made any plans. There hadn't been any tears, not even any good-byes. I hadn't asked him for anything, and he hadn't volunteered.

Nothing promised, so no promises broken. We were rebels. Outlaws. Outsiders. Standing at the end of my mother's driveway, I remembered something he had once said to me. That I was a

woman, and that he was a man, and that was all it took to make the
world go around. That was his philosophy.

My mother's little silver trailer was parked on the Lettesworth
side of the river, near the bridge. I knocked on the door for a full
ten minutes before she answered it. She wasn't happy to see me,
but when she learned that I was stranded, she shook her head and
let me in.

Melissa was there. That was the most important thing. Melissa
was a beautiful little girl, four years old, and it was wonderful to see
her and love her, but the agony of not having her—and of not feeling worthy of her—was just as bad as ever. Maybe worse.

When I held her in my arms, all the toughness and forgetfulness I'd tried to build into myself the past few years seemed to peel
right off and expose the pathetic person underneath. Instead of
straightening out my life since I'd lost her, I'd fallen even further
behind. I couldn't go back to that life, but I had no money and no
place to go forward to.

I couldn't stay where I was, either. To tell you how my mother
and I got along in that trailer home would be to retell the whole
story of our lives together. While I took care of Melissa and played
with her, she went out. When she'd return, after a few drinks and
maybe a visit to one of her boyfriends, she'd tell me in great detail
how I was mistreating my own child. We fought every old fight
again. All the old arguments and accusations and hatreds came
back.

I didn't want Melissa to see me this way. I didn't want to leave
Melissa with my mother, either, but I felt too weak and shameful to
steal her.

The way out of town presented itself in its usual manner.

On a hot Sunday afternoon an uncle of mine, Uncle Freddy,
came over from his house in Simmesport and invited me to go to the
carnival with him. Probably he just wanted to give my mother and
me a rest. Everybody in the family knew how badly we got along.

The Bluegrass Carnival—its name was painted on some of the
attractions—was parked in a wide spot by the side of the road. The
Bluegrass Carnival might not have gone over so well in a big city,
but for Lettesworth it was quite a bit to look at: a few thrill rides,

something called a Motor Dome—a big metal ball, inside of which a motorcyclist in a leather costume, a helmet, and goggles, drove around and around and finally upside down—a little midway with games of chance and dancing girls, and a strange-looking old tent that was covered with paintings of monsters and dinosaurs.

Uncle Freddy and I, and some of my Louisiana cousins, spent a few hours eating and drinking and riding the rides. By late afternoon I'd wandered away from my relatives and was sitting on a tree stump next to the funny-looking tent, waiting to go home. The tent was closed, its entrance flap tied shut. I'd seen everything else at the carnival, so I untied the tent and went inside. The tent was filled with animals: farm animals mostly, as well as I could make out, but there was also a dog or two and a strange-looking snake in a jar. All the live animals looked like they hadn't been fed or had their stalls cleaned in at least a day or two. As hot as it was outside, it was hotter in there. The smell was awful.

I went back outside, as quietly as I could, thinking, God, I'd like a beer. So I went over to the beer stand to get one. The next thing I knew, a woman I'd never seen before was standing at my side.

I hadn't even noticed her coming up to me. But she grabbed my arm and talked to me as if I were a long lost friend.

"How'd you like our little animal show?" she asked.

"It's okay, I guess."

"Well, then, how'd you like to run it? The girl who used to work it just quit."

I looked at her more closely. There was something about her— in some strange way, she did know me.

"Well, girl, I'm looking for a job."

She smiled, as if she'd known what I was going to say before I'd even said it.

"Do you know how to count?" she asked me.

"Sure," I said, "and I can add and subtract, too. I'm really educated. I could probably even multiply and divide for the right money."

She looked me over, up and down, and smiled. "You'll do fine," she said.

She pointed me toward a man in a hat and a leather vest, standing next to a trailer. Another person whose tired eyes saw too far into me.

"Do you know how to count?" he said, too. I gave him the same answer I'd given the woman, and he told me that if I wanted to, I could join up with them and run the freak show.

"All right," I said.

I asked him how much money I would make. He told me. It wasn't much, but it was better than nothing.

Thinking back, I suppose the man in the leather vest must have been running the carnival. Or then again, maybe not. I never really found out what his job was. In fact, I don't think he ever told me his name.

After a little while, Uncle Freddy came over to tell me that we were going back home now, but I told him I wasn't coming with him. He scratched his head, said good-bye, and left.

That was it. I was running the freak show at the Bluegrass Carnival. The motorcycle man who rode inside the Motor Dome took me aside, recited the freak show spiel four or five times, and by that evening I was standing in front of the tent, talking into a microphone and doing it myself. I was nervous as hell, but I was doing it. I could still do it today.

The pitch was as old as the carnival. Or even as old as the whole idea of carnivals. It was almost like a prayer. But it worked for me: by seven o'clock I had sold all of my roll of tickets. I had to go over to the trailer for more.

This is the freak show spiel, as it always was and always will be:

"Hurry, hurry, hurry! Step right up, ladies and gentlemen! See the mysteries of life explained to you, right behind this canvas door! See! The giant rat from Sumatra! See! The five-legged steer from Zanzibar! See! Why the elements of nature have put two heads on the body of a snake! Hey! Bring your wife over here and bring your little kid over here. Don't you want to know why these animals are like this? Do you wonder why God has bestowed on them these unworldly characteristics? Hurry, hurry, hurry! Step right up! See the freaks of nature! See why Mother Nature has chosen these animals to be this way!

"Don't you want to know the answer to life's mysteries? It's educational! Bring the kids! See the elephant-skinned dog! Step right up and see the two-headed snakes! Two heads with one body! Now, you married people know all about or what it would be like to have two heads with just one body!

"So hurry, hurry, hurry! See everything made clear to you! Come right inside! For just a mere two bits, two bits, twenty-five cents, one-quarter of a dollar! Step right up! Hurry! Hurry! Hurry!"

In a few days it was almost like I was regular carny. Which I suppose I was, because most of the people who worked with me worked just as long as they needed to—to get some money, or to get out of town, or to figure out what made them join up in the first place. Then, without making any fuss, they slipped away, back to their old life. Or to an entirely new one.

The carnies were some of the gentlest and most compassionate people I'd ever met. They weren't all poor people down on their luck—we had doctors and lawyers and college professors. We had lots of businessmen whose businesses had gone under.

All the hootchy-cootchy girls, who danced in grass skirts and tiny bra tops, were registered nurses. They told me that they had seen enough death and suffering to last a lifetime. Once, we all rented a motel room together just to remember what a hot shower and a bed was like.

One woman wrote beautiful poetry. Another told me she'd seen her husband die one weekend, her daughter the next, and her son commit suicide soon afterwards. Some people had sold their homes and their cars and almost everything else they owned before joining the carnival.

What we all had in common was that we were damaged people, out of step with the nine-to-five world. Some of us looked okay on the outside. Some of us were heavily depressed or heavily into drugs or alcohol. But nobody asked too many questions or criticized anyone else. Because somehow, in our own little world, we had enough self-respect to watch out for one another. So even though we didn't look like much, and though most of the customers must have thought we were scum, the carnival hung together.

After midnight, when the marks—the customers—went home, we'd all sit around the carnival, talking and drinking and smoking dope. Then we'd all sleep in back of the carnival's flatbed trucks.

*   *   *

Every day was just about the same. We woke up late in the
morning and did our chores. Mine was to take care of the animals,
which I didn't mind, because I felt as if we all had something in
common.

We were all freaks of nature. The elephant-skinned dog was just
a poor old dog with no hair, some kind of skin condition. He
would go outside whenever he could to bask in the sun. The five-
legged calf had been born with a stumpy little extra limb. The two-
headed snake had been dead for a long time.

I fed everybody on a strict schedule—all except the snake—and
made sure they had enough water and clean straw and exercise.
They were sweet animals, and I named them, just for myself, after
movie stars. Henry Fonda was the elephant-skinned dog. Jeannette
McDonald was the five-legged steer. If the snake could talk and if it
were alive, I was absolutely sure it would sound like Lauren Bacall,
so I called one head Lauren. The other head was Humphrey, of
course.

Every week or so the carnival would slough—which is pro-
nounced "slaw"—the carny word for breaking down the show and
moving on. It all got done smoothly, with hardly anybody telling
anyone what they needed to do. It was almost like a dream. All the
tents and rides and concession stands came apart like jigsaw puz-
zles, they were loaded on the trucks, and we'd ride down the road.

For the first few weeks after I signed on, we played in little
towns in Louisiana and Mississippi. Then we stopped for a while in
the parking lot of the Gator Bowl in Jacksonville, Florida.

Then, suddenly, the carnival season was over and I ended up in
the Bluegrass Carnival's winter quarters, which was just a piece of
blacktop in a ragtag neighborhood outside Fort Lauderdale.

In winter quarters nobody was paid or fed. We were welcome to
hang around and sleep on the trucks, though, and for lack of a
place to go to that was what I did. After two weeks, smoking and
drinking with the carnies who hadn't drifted away, I was down to
thirty dollars, a pair of clean bluejeans and two clean blouses, and
a lot of free time to think about things.

There was more than enough time to realize that I hadn't had
my period for a while. And that I was feeling headachy and nau-

seous each morning. Finally, even I couldn't deny the truth to myself.

I was pregnant. I was pregnant with my third child, even though I'd given up my other two. I was a deadbeat, a bum, a twenty-one-year old nobody at the end of my rope.

I was carrying the child who would become the *Roe* baby. How did I feel? That's what everybody who follows the story up to this point asks me. They're surprised when I tell them I wasn't really scared. I wasn't really depressed, either. I was down too low to feel the pain or shame that was stored up inside me.

In other words, I was outside the range of normal human feeling. Past really caring. Numb. At the time, I thought that was a good thing. But in time I would learn that I was very wrong.

"Norma, you've got to get a *plan* for yourself, girl."

One of my carny friends was squatting on his heels and frowning up at me. I'd told him what my problem was, and this was his advice. It was everyone's advice. It was well meaning, but it didn't do me any good. It was time for me to slip away.

I'd made some tries to get waitress work in the neighborhood. But none of the restaurants seemed to be hiring pregnant redneck hippie carnies from Texas. The only solution, dim as it was, was to get back to Dallas.

I went to a nearby store and changed a bunch of my dollars into coins. This bunch of loose change, I knew, was my last lifeline. I pushed the coins into a pay phone and called every gay bar in Dallas whose name I could remember. When I got through I'd ask if anyone in the place knew Pixie.

At a place called the Rendezvous someone finally did. A friend of mine named Carla said she would wire me the difference between the money I had and the price of a bus ticket from Florida.

I rode the bus back to Dallas with three dollars and two packs of cigarettes in my pocket. The ride must have lasted only a couple of days, but it seemed to take weeks. I changed clothes in bus stations along the way. In the Houston Greyhound station I took a bath underneath my clothes—washing with soap and water underneath my dirty blouse and then stripping it off, drying myself with paper towels, and putting on a fresh blouse before anyone could see me.

Somebody must have, though, because when I came out of the ladies' room a bus company guard grabbed my arm, took my name, and told me in no uncertain terms that if I ever did that again, in this or any other bus station on the Greyhound system, I would be arrested. I got back on the bus for the last leg of my trip. Between hours of feeling dead tired and sick to my stomach, I did come up with a plan: I wouldn't go back to Renee or sell drugs again. No. The police were probably looking for me already. Instead I would find my father, who I'd heard had broken up with May and moved out of her apartment house, and move in with him. Then I'd go on from there.

That was as far as my thinking went. When the bus reached Dallas even those thoughts melted away. Being back in town, in far worse shape than when I'd left, was so depressing that it seemed to cut the connection between myself and all the other people in the world. After all, how could I face anyone? What could I tell them? What was my explanation? What excuse did I have for taking up space on this earth at all?

I was so tired and low that my brain slowed down. I couldn't remember what my plan was. I couldn't make a decision. I couldn't even get myself to leave the Dallas bus station. I wandered around inside it for five days, sleeping in the waiting room and buying a candy bar when I remembered to eat.

Finally, somehow, a sense of what I was doing to myself, of how fast I was falling, began to sink in. Something broke me out of my trance. I had a vision—of the women at the Rendezvous gathered around the bar drinking. They were talking to each other, enjoying themselves. Laughing. I put a dime in the phone and dialed the bar's number. The manager, Roz,[*] answered.

"Hi, it's Pixie," I said, as normally as I could. "What's happening?"

Roz asked me where I was. I told her. I also told her how long I'd been there. She said she would send someone in her car to pick me up.

A woman named Jinx—everybody called her that—was the person who met me at the bus station. Jinx was a big, friendly looking woman. A great softball player, a good heart. She was a nurse's aide. She died a few years ago of cirrhosis of the liver.

That morning, after she drove me to the bar, Jinx took one look at me and drove me over to the house where she lived with her mother. She told me to take a shower and clean myself up, and then she would come and get me. Jinx's mother, a real down-home country Texan, cooked me up a big breakfast of eggs and bacon. With my stomach full of food, I began to feel halfway close to normal. I mopped up the last bit of breakfast with a piece of toast.

"You're pregnant, aren't you, sweetie?" said Jinx's mother.

"How can you tell?" I asked.

She smiled sadly, shook her head, and held out her arms. I walked around the table and cried on her shoulder for a long time—for the first time in a long time.

I used her phone to call a friend of my father's. He said he didn't have a clue as to where Jimmy Nelson was, but he would put out the word that his daughter was looking for him. Later that afternoon Jinx came back and drove me to the bar. Later that evening, Roz pulled me aside and said that if I wanted it, there was a job open for a weekend bartender.

"Yeah, okay, I'm interested," I told her. I tried to put on a mask and act a little tough, as if I had other job offers lining up outside on the street, waiting for me. She was good-natured enough to ignore this part.

"Okay, Pixie," she said, "you can start right now." She added that it would be good if I moved into an apartment across the street. She would advance me the money for my first month's rent.

I settled into my old routine, sleeping during the day and taking as many shifts as I could. On my nights off I went to the Rendezvous as a customer, or to other bars. It was almost like the old days.

Except that I couldn't fool myself into turning back the clock. In the past few years I'd been down too far. It had given me too much knowledge of myself. I knew now that there was something very wrong with me.

I was damaged goods. For the moment, I had control of myself and knew where my next meal was coming from. But I also knew there was something dark and scary waiting for me—or maybe already inside me. Something drugs or beer or running couldn't make go away.

There was a baby. No, not a baby. I couldn't even bear to think of it as that. There was this thing growing inside of me, getting bigger every day, and I couldn't push the terrible fact of it out of my mind. This wasn't like the other times. I didn't want to give birth to another unwanted child. I didn't want to have to give up another child. I didn't want a child to be born with me as its mother.

There was no good reason to bring this poor thing into the world. I simply didn't want to be pregnant. *I didn't want to be pregnant.*

"You don't want to have this baby? Why don't you get rid of it?" said the customer across the bar.

Get rid of it?

It was a night at the bar just like any other night. Like a hundred other nights. Music, pool, smoke. Drinking Lone Star on tap. Or Schlitz. Or Bud. Or margaritas. Or mimosas.

Mostly regulars, a few newcomers. Everyone was careful around newcomers. The woman was someone I'd seen around. I'd been serving her for a while, talking back and forth and pouring out my troubles, but when she said that I shut up and thought for a moment. Get rid of it? Get rid of it?

How?

I moved away from the customer. I didn't want to show her my astonishment. My ignorance, really. Anyway, I thought, she just might be too drunk to be making any sense. So I let it drop. Later, I grabbed ahold of Jinx:

"Can you believe what that girl over there told me? She said I didn't have to be pregnant anymore. She said if I didn't want to have a baby, I could just get rid of it."

Jinx looked at me as if I was crazy.

"Sure. Get rid of it. Why not?" she said. My heart started pounding. Was there actually a way out of this? Could I actually put a stop to my pregnancy?

"Oh, Pixie," said Jinx, seeing the shocked look on my face, and realizing, "didn't you know that doctors can stop a woman from being pregnant?"

"No," I said.

"Well, hell, girl," said Jinx, "they do it all the time."

"All the time?"

"Sure," said Jinx, walking away. A kind of hysteria got hold of me. For the rest of the night I was so happy I was in a state of shock. I went through the motions of working, but inside I was somewhere else. *There was a way to get unpregnant. Doctors did it for their patients. All the time.* For those few hours, I was in heaven. There was an answer to my problem. Doctors did it! I could see my way out. I could feel it. My doctor would do it to me, and I could start my life all over again. Doctors did it.

The next morning I called Dr. Brady,* the man who had delivered my two babies.

Dr. Brady's nurse told me that since the last time I had seen him, the doctor had left gynecology and obstetrics and gone into radiology. What that meant, she explained, was that he was taking X-rays now instead of delivering babies.

"That's all right," I said. "I just want to ask him a question. An important one."

"Well . . . okay," said the nurse. She gave me a few phone numbers where he might be reached. I called all of them from the pay phone in the bar, leaving my name and number each time. I stayed close to the phone, chain smoking, almost vibrating, waiting for a callback. A few hours later, he called.

"What's the problem, Norma?" he said.

Dr. Brady sounded as if he was in a hurry. But that was all right. I just needed a minute or two of his time. The important thing was to make myself very clear.

"Dr. Brady, I'm pregnant again."

"Well, Norma," he said, "you've been pregnant before. What's the matter?"

"Dr. Brady, I don't want to do this. I don't want the pregnancy. I don't want the child. I don't want to be pregnant. Now, I just heard that there's something you can do to not be pregnant. Only, I don't know what it's called."

He had an answer for me in a second.

"Oh, you want to abort," he said.

"What?"

"You want an abortion," he said, a little impatiently.

"I guess I do," I said, trying to keep down my excitement. "What exactly is it?"

At this, he began to sound even busier.

"Listen, Norma. I've got to go now. Why don't you look it up in the dictionary?"

He hung up.

I asked Jinx if she had a dictionary in the bar, and she looked at me as if I'd lost my mind. I went to a bar across the street—and, believe it or not, they had one.

I looked up "abortion" and found out that it meant just what I thought it did. The next day I called Dr. Brady's nurse again and said I wanted an appointment to see the doctor.

She tried to put me off, telling me that Dr. Brady didn't see patients like me anymore. But I was so persistent, telling her that I'd hold forever while she took all her other calls, that she finally gave me a time when I could go see him in his office.

The appointment was three days away. In my ignorance, I was as happy during those three days as I'd been in a long time.

Dr. Brady, in his spotless white coat, leaned against the wall of his examining room and looked at me sadly. Very sadly.

Why?

"Norma, I don't do abortions. And I don't know anyone who does. In fact, if I heard of anyone who was doing them, I'd have to report them to the AMA."

What? The AMA? What was that? And who cared?

"What do you mean I can't have an abortion?" I said. "I want one. Doctors do it. I'll pay you for it."

He shook his head. As I sat there, stunned, he explained, slowly and gently as if I were a little child, that abortion was illegal in Texas. It had always been illegal in Texas, and it would probably continue to be illegal in Texas.

"Then you can't give me one?"

"No, Norma. I'm sorry."

"Then who can?"

He just hook his head again.

"Norma, I'm sorry."

In that instant, my happiness turned completely inside out on itself, into fear. I tried to fight it. I needed to get out of this god-damn doctor's office. The most awful question was sinking in: If he couldn't tell me how to get an abortion, who could?

"Norma," said Dr. Brady, "you really should have taken care of yourself. You really should have thought about this before you went and got pregnant again."

I didn't say anything. I was disappointed and angry all at one time. My fear was already turning into despair. I started to cry—as much out of frustration and shame at my own ignorance and powerlessness as from disappointment.

Dr. Brady leaned forward. "Listen, Norma," he said softly, "have you considered putting up the child for adoption? Don't you think that you should give this child to a loving couple who can't have children? Don't you think that that's the best way to go?"

"No! I can't do that again!" I yelled. "I want an abortion!" He sighed, looked down, and pulled over his prescription pad in front of him and began to write.

For just a second, my heart leapt up into my throat.

He's changed his mind, I thought. He's taken pity on me. He's going to give me a prescription, or write out an order, or do whatever he had to do for me to get an abortion.

He handed me the piece of paper. On it was a phone number. "Norma, I want you to call this man," he said.

"Is this a doctor?"

"No. It's a lawyer I know who handles adoptions," he said. "I want you to get in touch with him as soon as possible." I walked back to the bar in shock.

"Well, hell, Pixie, of course they're not legal," said Jinx.

She explained it to me. For some reason, she said, stopping a pregnancy was considered a crime, like murder. It didn't make much sense—actually, the rule against abortions was a Christian religious law that had somehow crossed over into the legal system. But there was no use arguing. If the police found out that you'd had or done an abortion, you could be arrested.

But not everybody believed that abortions should be stopped. In fact, most people didn't. That's why there were doctors—and people who weren't doctors, also—who did abortions in secret. They could get arrested at any moment if they were discovered. So it stood to reason that they couldn't let it get out in public that they were doing them. It was up to the women who needed abortions to find these people themselves.

"But how?" I said.

"I don't know exactly, but there are ways," said Jinx. The important thing, said Jinx, is to be careful.

"You've got to get somebody who knows what they're doing. Otherwise, if somebody does it in the wrong way, you can get hurt really bad. Or even die."

"Well, Jinx, do you know anybody who does abortions?"

She looked a little surprised—no, a little scared, when I asked her that.

"I'm sorry, Pixie, I don't," she said. "You'll just have to find one yourself."

"Listen," I said, leaning over to talk to a woman, a little older than me, who'd been coming in three or four nights a weeks since I'd worked at the Rendezvous, "do you know where I can get an abortion?"

She shook her head no, squirmed in her seat, and looked down into her drink.

This was no surprise. Nobody at the bar—at least the ones I felt comfortable enough asking—knew where I could go to get an abortion. And worse, I was deathly afraid of asking anyone else. The idea of letting strangers know that I wanted to do something illegal set off every alarm bell in my head. So I stopped asking them. And when I stopped to think about it, I got furious that somewhere women were getting abortions, and I was still in the dark.

The only clue I had, if you could call it that, was the phone number that Dr. Brady had given me. That lawyer was a middle-aged man in a three-piece suit. I sat in his downtown office in my best jeans and blouse. He didn't smile or shake my hand. He read my name off a piece of paper on his desk and then looked at me as if I were a piece of dirt underneath his heel. I knew I'd made a mistake the moment our eyes met. I wanted to get up and run out of that office. Instead, because he was my only hope, I kept going.

I told him I wanted an abortion. He stared at me for a second, shook his head, and told me he certainly couldn't help me get one. He knew nothing about abortions.

"I handle adoptions," he said. He pulled out another piece of paper, unscrewed his pen, and asked me a list of questions.

"How far along are you?"

I told him.

"How did you get pregnant?"

"How do you think?" I said.

He looked at me again. Now I was even lower than dirt.

"Were you raped?" he asked me.

Time stopped. Was I raped? A flash of the man who had raped me so many years ago. I pushed the picture out of my mind. Why is he asking me this? I wondered. Then I thought, Maybe this is a trick question. Maybe if I had been raped, *surely* if I had been raped, it would make me an exception to the rule against getting an abortion.

"Yes," I lied.

He stared at me.

"What color was the man who raped you?"

What kind of question was that? I thought.

"Excuse me?" I said.

"What color was the man who raped you?"

Things were getting out of control. I felt dirty, ashamed, and angry. I shouldn't have lied. Now he was punishing me.

"I don't know," I said quickly. "It was too dark to tell."

At that point the lawyer seemed to get even colder.

"We're almost finished," he said.

As I sat there in his leather chair, trembling, he double-checked my address and phone number. Then he said that he would let me know his decision, then told me I could leave. I managed to control myself long enough to get out the door.

A few days later, Dr. Brady called me at the bar. He told me that the lawyer he'd referred me to had called him. This man had told him that he couldn't help me because he felt that my baby was probably of mixed race and would be hard to place with white parents.

I was too stunned to say anything. Dr. Brady said that I shouldn't give up hope. He knew another lawyer who might help me.

He made me write down this other man's number. I thanked him for his help, hung up the phone, and began to cry and curse at the same time.

∽ 10 ∽

That was, I guess, a turning point. In the next few weeks I went nearly out of my mind with anger and panic. I did everything I could to change my situation. Some of the things I did were sane, some weren't. Because I was so angry and terrified, I couldn't have told you which ones were which. By this time the Rendezvous had changed hands, and I didn't get along well with the new owner. By this time, too, even Pixie McCorvey suspected that working in a bar wasn't the perfect job for a pregnant woman. So I quit. I spent my days at my father's place, keeping it clean for him and making him his dinner each night.

The only person on my side, I figured, was my father. He had heard that I was looking for him, finally, and had given me a call. I went over to visit him. He was living in a new apartment. I told him how lonely it was living by myself. He said that he felt the same way, and that it would be all right with him if I moved in.

It was the best thing that had happened to me in a very long time. I gave up my apartment and began keeping house for my father. But as far as finding an abortion—I didn't dare ask him, either.

I became friendly with an old woman who lived in my father's building. After a few days I asked her if she knew where I could find an abortion doctor. She said she didn't—but that I didn't really need one. She'd heard that drinking a bottle of castor oil and eating a few pounds of peanuts would bring on an abortion all by itself.

The next day I went to the store, bought everything I needed, forced myself to swallow all of it, and made myself as sick to my stomach as I'd ever been. I thought I was going to die. After awhile, I hoped I would.

But I didn't die. Which, even when I felt a little better, I wasn't sure was the absolute best outcome.

Because the next afternoon, when I started to feel myself again, it was a self who was still pregnant. And who was going to have a baby, even if it killed her.

Now I was back to the beginning. No, it was worse than that. The only thing I could think of doing was calling the second lawyer whose name Dr. Brady had given me. Which meant that I was down to this choice: facing another heartless man, and letting him treat me like a piece of garbage, or admitting that I was absolutely helpless, that I could do absolutely nothing to stop my pregnancy.

I made my decision and called the number.

I was ready to hang up on him in a second. But much to my surprise, the man who answered—no secretary—seemed sympathetic. This lawyer had a gentle voice, friendly and concerned at the same time. When I told him what my problem was, he asked me to come down to his office when it was convenient for me.

In person, Henry McCluskey looked as much like a gentleman as he sounded. He had a mustache. He dressed neatly, in a jacket and tie, but not as conservatively as the other lawyer. He asked me all about myself and listened to my whole story sympathetically. He seemed genuinely interested in me as a person, not just someone carrying a baby he could sell.

(I later learned that Henry was gay, like me, but deeply in the closet. Linda Coffee, one of the two lawyers on the *Roe* case, was the woman he dated to keep up appearances. A few years ago, this dear man was murdered by a man whom he had broken up with.)

The only damn problem was that, although he was much nicer to me, his answer was the same.

"Norma," he said, sadly, "you know that abortions are illegal in Texas, don't you?"

"I don't care about that," I said. "Can't you put me in touch with a doctor who does them, anyway?"

Now he looked even sadder. "Absolutely not," he said.

"Then why do I feel you're lying to me?" I said, starting to get angry.

He changed the subject right away. Like Dr. Brady, he tried to talk me into thinking that giving my baby to another woman would be a wonderful thing for me to do.

I told him of another fear I'd had recently—that my baby would be given to a mother who thought she couldn't bear children, but who managed to get pregnant with her own child after she'd taken my baby.

"What kind of treatment would my child get then?" I said.

We went back and forth on this subject for a while. Finally, Henry sighed and turned straight to me.

"Do you feel that strongly about getting an abortion?"

"Yes," I said. "And with or without you, I'm going to get one. Wherever I can find it."

At this point Henry got distressed. Even a little angry himself, in a concerned sort of way. He looked me straight in the eye. He told me that illegal abortions were dangerous, very dangerous, and that lots of women got killed when they had them.

"I don't care," I said.

Henry McCluskey thought for a second, came to some sort of decision, looked at me, and said the most important words I'd hear in my entire life:

"Norma," he said, "I know a couple of young lawyers who are looking for a pregnant woman who wants an abortion. A woman just like you. The reason is, they need her to be a plaintiff in a lawsuit, to help them overturn the Texas law against abortions."

"Will it help me get an abortion?" I asked Henry.

"To be honest with you, Norma," he said, "I don't know."

For a few seconds, I thought about what he'd just said. If I had been ready to be completely honest with Henry, I would have told him I had very little idea of what he was talking about. From what I could figure out, though, what he was talking about had more to do with solving his friends' problem than mine.

Before I left, I gave him my father's address and phone number. I told him I would think about his proposition.

*   *   *

I went to the Dallas Free Clinic for a pregnancy test. The result was no surprise. Neither was the answer I got when I asked the doctor if he knew where I could get an abortion.

On my way out, though, the woman at the front desk whispered to me that she knew of a place where they did abortions. My heart started to beat faster.

"Where?" I asked, not even daring to hope that this stranger had solved my problem.

She told me the address. It was at the corner of West Davis and Tyler streets, in the Oak Cliff section of Dallas.

I kept calm. I didn't dare get my hopes up too high. I took the bus to Oak Cliff. The abortion building was a small, low, windowless place with a sign out in front that said DENTIST. The strange thing was that the front door was cracked open. I screwed up my courage and pushed my way in.

"Hello?" I said.

There was nobody inside. I suddenly realized this wasn't a dentist's office. But beyond that I didn't know where I was. Except that I was in a nightmare. One that I didn't really understand—or was afraid to.

What I saw first was an old, old wooden doctor's examining table sitting abandoned in the middle of a big room. The table was dirty. Filthy. So was the whole office. There was dried blood on the floor. And on the examining table. Regular tables and chairs and filing cabinets were scattered on the floor, overturned as if there had been a big fight a few minutes ago.

The place smelled horrible. The odor was overpowering. It was ten times worse than anything I had ever smelled before. I'd never smelled anything like it, but somehow I knew what it was. I got sick to my stomach. I ran outside and threw up in the alley.

I hadn't seen a single person during the time I was inside. But then, out of the corner of my eye, I saw a man. A rough-looking, streetwise-looking man. He was standing nearby, no real expression on his face, just watching me throw up.

"What's the matter?" he said.

I straightened up and turned toward him. "I thought. . . ?" It was all I could say.

"Oh, yeah," he said. "They all got busted last week."

Then he walked away.

I looked around again, this time more carefully. There was a police sawhorse sitting next to the building. There were pieces of police crime scene tape lying on the ground next to it. A crime scene! That thought scared me almost as much as what I'd seen inside. I pulled myself together as best I could, went home and double-locked the door behind me.

The next day I called Henry McCluskey and told him to pass on my name.

I suppose it would be nice to say here that when I made that phone call—after which a woman named Linda Coffee called me back to set up a meeting—I realized I was making abortion-rights history. Or changing my life forever.

But the honest truth is that nothing like that even occurred to me. I was simply at the end of my rope. At a dead end. I just didn't know what else to do.

∽11∽

In February 1970 I was Norma McCorvey, a pregnant street person. A twenty-one-year-old woman in big trouble. I became Jane Roe at a corner table at Columbo's, an Italian restaurant at Mockingbird Lane and Greenville Avenue, in Dallas. I'd suggested to Linda Coffee that we meet there.

Columbo's is gone now, which is a shame. It was an inexpensive place, clean, and made very good pizza. The tables had red-and-white checked tablecloths—just like the one I'd bought for Woody back in California. Columbo's wasn't very big. When I walked into the place that evening, I didn't have any trouble figuring out who was waiting for me.

Linda Coffee and Sarah Weddington, sitting together, stood out in Columbo's. Both were older than me, and both were wearing two-piece business suits. Nice clothing, expensive looking. One of them was tall and dark and thin. Delicate. The other was short and blond and a little plump, her hair in a stiff-looking permanent. Her hairdo was old-fashioned, even for then.

I was wearing jeans, a button-down shirt tied at the waist, and sandals. I wore my bandanna tied around my left leg, above the knee. That meant I didn't have a girlfriend.

I walked over to their table. It was obvious to me even from across the room that these women hadn't talked to a person like me for a long time, if ever. For a second, I felt like turning around and running out the door, writing the whole meeting off and starting over again. But I didn't. Instead, I thought, Norma, they're just as scared of you as you are of them. Looking at the nervousness and doubt in their eyes, I almost believed it.

"Hi. I'm Norma McCorvey?" I said.

The shorter blond woman came to life.

"I'm Sarah Weddington," she said.

Sarah Weddington reached out and shook my hand. Linda introduced herself, too, but it was apparent right away that Sarah was the one who would speak for both of them. For most of that meeting—in fact, for most of all our meetings—it was Sarah who talked, and it was Sarah who listened to me with the most concentration.

"Thanks for showing up," I said.

I don't remember much else about the first few minutes. Small talk was awkward for us, considering how little we had in common. I talked about Henry and how much I liked him. Sarah agreed. She told me that she and Linda were lawyers, which I already knew. The conversation died down.

I went to order our pizza and beer at the counter. While I stood there, waiting, I worked up the courage to ask these women the only question I was interested in getting an answer to.

I brought the beer back to the table.

"Do you know where I can get an abortion?" I said.

"No," said Sarah, "I don't."

Son of a bitch! I thought. I sat up in my chair and got ready to leave. I didn't want to hear the adoption spiel again.

But surprisingly, Sarah didn't begin to give it to me. Instead—and this is what kept me from leaving—she went off in another direction entirely.

"Norma, do you really want an abortion?" she asked.

"Yes," I said.

"Why?"

"Because I don't want this baby. I don't even figure it's a baby. And I figure it's making my life pretty miserable, right now."

"Yes," said Sarah. "Go on."

I looked closely at her to see if what I'd said disgusted her. Or made her dislike me. But no, all I could see was that she was interested in my story. And maybe, just maybe, interested in helping me somehow.

"See, Sarah," I said, "my being pregnant, I don't think I'll be able to find work. And if I can't get work I can't take care of myself. I don't want to be pregnant. I don't want this *thing* growing inside my body!"

By the end of my answer I was almost shouting. But Sarah didn't seem to mind.

"Norma," she said, "do you know what the abortion process is? Do you know what women have to go through when they get one?"

"Not really," I admitted. "But I kind of have a general idea."

Sarah told me, roughly, what a doctor did during a regular abortion. It sounded awful. But the truth was, it wasn't much different from what I had imagined all along.

Sarah leaned forward. "Norma. Don't do you think woman should have access to abortions? Safe, legal abortions?"

For the first time I realized that Sarah and Linda weren't just ordinary lawyers. For the first time I realized how interested she was in what *I* was interested in. Abortions. And in my getting one, too? Despite everything, my hopes rose a little.

"Sure," I said, "of course they should. But there aren't any legal ones around. So I guess I've got to find an illegal one, don't I?"

"No!" said Sarah and Linda, together.

"Why the hell not?" I said.

I felt a little flare of anger. First they were for abortions. Then they didn't want me to have one. What kind of mind games were these women playing with me?

"Because they're dangerous, Norma," said Sarah. "Illegal abortions are dangerous."

"Yeah, so?" I said.

Sarah shook her head. Then this woman in her nice suit, a woman I couldn't have imagined even going to a horror movie, began to tell me stories.

Terrible stories. Stories of women who'd had illegal abortions and lived to regret them. Or hadn't lived. Women who'd gone to gangsters, or shady doctors, and had their insides torn out. And who'd gone home and bled to death.

"These women were murdered," said Sarah. Then she told me about pregnant, unmarried women who had been so desperate to get rid of their babies that they'd tried to give themselves abortions with coat hangers. And killed themselves.

Then the worst story—one that made me shiver with fear. Sarah told me about a woman who didn't want anyone to know she had gotten the abortion—who was found, in a pool of blood, in a hotel room in New York City.

"They didn't find her for a couple of days," said Sarah. "And even when they did, she had no identification. So they didn't know who she was. They couldn't notify her family. All they could do was call her Jane Doe. And wait for someone to come forward and claim her body."

Jane Doe! That could be me.

An awful picture passed through my mind. Of me, alone—no friends, no lovers, not even a name—lying dead in that hotel room. Who would claim my body?

I began to cry, in front of strangers. Smart, rich strangers, who made me feel poor and ignorant. It was awful that they were seeing me cry. Embarrassing. Sarah handed me a Kleenex from her purse.

"Yes," she said, "it's really unfair and inhuman. And it shouldn't have to happen to any woman. Rich or poor. Anywhere." That's why, she said, she and Linda and some other people who thought just like them were working hard to overturn the Texas law against abortions. Their weapon was a legal project, a lawsuit, to challenge the law in the courts.

She wasn't sure if they would be successful, but if they could do it—and it would take a lot of hard work, plus a pregnant women like me, who wanted but wasn't able to get an abortion, to put her name on their lawsuit—then abortions would be legal in the state of Texas.

"Would that mean that somebody like me would be able to get an abortion?" I said.

"Yes," said Sarah, "it would."

It would? New hope began to flood through me, even though I'd been crying my eyes out a few seconds ago.

"That would be great," I said, excited despite myself.

"Yes!" said Sarah, just as excitedly.

In her excitement, Sarah began describing the road the lawsuit would take—through district courts and appeals courts, state courts and federal courts. Early on, I lost the thread of what she was saying. But I kept nodding anyway. Sarah sounded so revved up, so intense, so passionate about her plans, that it was as if she were telling me her innermost personal secrets—instead of describing all sorts of complicated legal business, using words that I was certain only lawyers understood.

I thought, I don't really want to hear about courts. I've been in too many courts in my life. But I didn't want to interrupt her. This woman might be able to help me.

Finally, she stopped.

"That's great," I said, a little bit too late.

But I must not have fooled anybody, because there was an awkward silence. Then somebody, either Sarah or Linda, asked me to tell them all about myself.

Another silence. A longer one. All about myself? What would these woman think about me if I told them all about myself? I didn't know much—anything at all, really—about their lives, but I was pretty sure they hadn't gone to reform school or dealt drugs or been beaten by their husbands or spent their days and nights in gay bars.

They might be shocked—or worse, maybe disgusted—by my story. On the other hand, they seemed to like me, wanted to connect with me, in their own way.

Would they still want to help if me I told them that my private life was none of their damn business? I took a deep breath and made my decision.

Over that red checkered tablecloth, I told them everything. Or almost everything. Louisiana and Dallas and Woody McCorvey. The whole miserable story. Over pizza and a pitcher of beer. While the people at the next table laughed and whooped it up.

Sarah and Linda hung in and listened sympathetically for a while. Then I got to the part of telling them I was a lesbian. That I liked girls. That I lived with women, get it?

Sarah and Linda looked at each other. They frowned. I felt the flashes of fear and doubt and confusion passing between them. I realized what they were thinking: how could this woman who says she's a lesbian have gotten herself pregnant all these times? It doesn't make sense. Maybe nothing she's told us makes sense. But here's what does make sense: maybe she's lying to us. Or maybe there's something we don't understand about her. Something weird. Something dangerous. Something that will hurt our lawsuit. Hurt us.

No! Inside my head, I shouted back to them: You don't have to worry about my hurting you! I'm only dangerous to myself!

They didn't hear me. But how could I explain it all in words? I could sense them thinking about brushing me off and finding another pregnant woman. They were slipping away from me. And with them, my only chance for an abortion.

I panicked.

"You know," I said, "I was raped. That's how I became pregnant with this baby."

The horrible lie—this was the second time I'd used it—pulled at the insides of my stomach. But it got their attention. The two lawyers turned away from each other and quickly said they were sorry to hear this. That rape is a terrible thing. A crime.

"Was the rapist arrested?" asked Sarah.

"No," I said.

"Did the police look very hard for him?"

"No," I said, sinking deeper and deeper.

"Did you report the rape to the police?"

"No," I said, burning inside with shame.

Sarah stopped quizzing me. I tried to figure out whether she thought I was lying. This time, I couldn't read her.

She looked at Linda again. They seemed to come to some sort of conclusion.

"Well, Norma," she said, "it's awful that you were raped. But actually, the Texas abortion law doesn't make any exception for rape. So it doesn't matter in terms of our lawsuit."

"Oh, that's too bad," I said.

"Yes, it is," said Sarah.

A long pause.

"Well, anyway, we would like to have you as a plaintiff in our lawsuit. Would you like to help us?"

"Sure," I said, trying to be as cool as I could. A plaintiff. What was that? Well, I'd look it up in the dictionary later. At least I hadn't lost this chance.

We drank a beer toast to our lawsuit. Before she left, Sarah explained to me that they'd need me to sign some legal papers.

With my own name, if I wanted to, but under a false name if I wanted to stay anonymous.

"Great," I said.

Sarah asked me if I had any questions. I said yes, I did.

"How much will I have to pay you two for being my lawyers?" I said.

Sarah smiled. "Nothing, Norma. We're doing this case *pro bono*." That meant, she said, that they were doing it for free.

"Then when can I get my abortion?" I asked.

"When the case is over, if we've won," said Sarah.

I was two and a half months pregnant. I didn't know how late you could get an abortion, but I did know that it was better to do it as soon as possible. How long could a lawsuit take? I remembered some of the trials I'd seen on television. The times I'd been in court myself. None of those occasions seemed to have taken much time at all.

"When will that be?" I said.

Sarah looked at me closely. I can see her sitting across from me, right now.

"It's really impossible to tell you that, Norma," she said. "We'll just have to let due process take its course."

It was a couple of weeks until I heard from Sarah and Linda again. In the meantime, I stayed at my dad's. I didn't tell him, or anyone else, about what had happened at Columbo's. Why risk being held up to public ridicule if the whole thing failed and we lost, and I still had to have a baby? Or worse, what if it was all some kind of harebrained scheme—or even a scam?

That's what made me decide to stay anonymous. To not put my own name on the lawsuit.

By the time Linda called me to come down to her office I was cleaning my father's apartment immaculately, several times a day, as if I was possessed by cleaning demons. I went downtown, and in front of Sarah and Linda signed a piece of paper. Not as Jane Doe—that reminded me of the woman who had been killed giving herself an illegal abortion—but as Jane Roe. The whole thing took only a few minutes. Sarah and Linda seemed very excited about it all. And so was I, despite myself, despite the feeling that I shouldn't be getting my hopes up too high.

And that was the start of *Roe* v. *Wade.* The lawsuit that would allow me, and millions of other women, to be in control of our own destinies.

To me, it didn't feel historic. Just a little confusing . . . and intimidating.

I didn't even know who Wade—Henry Wade, the Dallas district attorney who would be fighting the lawsuit against us—was. But that was all right. Sarah and Linda looked as if they knew what they were doing.

They both thanked me and said I could go home and let them do the legal work.

And then I waited.

I waited for two months, although it seemed much longer. To be honest, I wasn't that comfortable talking to Linda and Sarah, so I didn't have much contact with them.

But Henry McCluskey and I got along fine. Henry called me every week or two, at my dad's house, and told me that the case was moving along. He asked me how I was holding up. He reminded me, every time we talked, that he would be glad to arrange an adoption if the lawsuit didn't work.

Poor Henry. He got an earful whenever he said that. That gentle man probably heard a lot more from Jane Roe than he'd bargained for. I don't think either of us really knew how bad a shape I was in. Or the storm that was coming toward us, just over the horizon.

It was a strange pregnancy. It was a strange time, watching and feeling this baby—no, this *thing* I didn't want happening to me—growing bigger and bigger inside me. Some days, I looked very pregnant. Others, for some reason, I didn't look pregnant at all. I was out of work. Alone most of the day in a little apartment. I had all the time in the world to think about things.

My moods swung up and down, usually by the day, sometimes by the hour. When I was up, I was way up—I was the smartest thing on two legs. I wasn't just sitting around feeling sorry for myself, after all—I had taken action. I'd gotten a pair of wonderful smart young lawyers, and I was going to win my case and be the first girl in Texas to get a legal abortion.

But that great feeling didn't last long. When I was down, I went way down—down into depths of doubt and despair, for hour after empty hour.

"What's actually happening, Norma?" I asked myself.

"Here's what," I answered. "You're in trouble. Bad trouble. You're four months pregnant, broke and alone. You're a bad mother. You've lost touch with both of your children."

I was lower than low. Between a rock and a hard place. If I knew anything at all, I knew I couldn't survive having another child—I couldn't take care of it, and I couldn't give it up, either.

My only hope was to get an abortion. But the only way I could get an abortion was by trusting these two women, women I didn't really know, to take my case through the courts, where no good had ever come to me. I'd signed a piece of paper. So what? No piece of paper had ever helped me before.

Nothing could help me. And why? Because basically, I was no good. So that meant that no good would come of anything I ever did. The lawsuit had my signature on it—that meant it was doomed.

And me? Maybe I was doomed, too. Maybe it would be best if I just ran away. Or got out of the way. By throwing myself down a flight of stairs. Or trying one of those fatal self-abortions that Sarah had talked about. Or maybe. . .

Or maybe, when the dark clouds eventually lifted a little, I shouldn't just sit here waiting. I had to move, keep ahead of the bad thoughts. It was sitting in the apartment all by myself, I decided, that was doing this to me. My solution wasn't tremendously original.

To stay ahead of the demons I hitchhiked to Oaklawn, the part of Dallas where all the hippies hung out. This was the full flowering of the Age of Aquarius—at least for Dallas it was. Everyone wore bell-bottoms and tie-dyed T-shirts.

Renee wasn't around anymore. The people on the street were passive, laid-back, relaxed—calm. They shared their dope and they read me the poetry they'd just written. Nobody asked me how I'd gotten pregnant, or what I was going to do about it.

The next thing I knew I was sleeping in a crash pad with a bunch of friendly people who liked me very much. The next thing after that, I was moving out of my father's house. He said that if that's what I wanted to do, it was fine with him.

I discovered that if I smoked enough dope and drank enough wine, it was possible to not think about being pregnant, which was good. I just had to keep in touch with Henry. In a few weeks—it might have been three or even four—I decided the time was right to call him.

Henry, of course, was frantic.

"Where have you been?" he said. "We've been trying to get in touch with you."

"Well, Henry," I told him, "here I am."

Henry said that he and Linda and Sarah had been desperately looking for me everywhere. My father, and everybody else they could thing of contacting, either couldn't or wouldn't tell them where I was.

Henry told me that my case was going to trial right away— "Great!" I said. "That means it's almost over!"—but that before the actual trial began I would have to sign some papers, my "affidavit," whatever that was.

I hitched a ride to Linda's office. I signed the papers. Both she and Sarah took good long looks at my bulging belly. We decided together that it probably wasn't too good an idea for me to sit in on the trial. So while they argued against Henry Wade, I went back to Oaklawn.

I was invisible again. And I stayed invisible, burying myself in drugs in alcohol, as Linda and Sarah made history in my name.

I was six months pregnant by the time the trial was over. When I called in, Linda told me to come right over. She sounded excited. After I finally arrived, hot and tired, she said that she had both good news and bad news to tell me. The good news was that we had won the case.

"That's wonderful," I said, holding my breath for the second part.

The bad news was that I had lost.

Even though the judges had ruled that abortion was now legal in Texas, Henry Wade had announced he would appeal the case—

and until that appeal was decided, he would prosecute any doctor who performed an abortion on a woman.

"Well, then, Linda, how long will the appeal take?" I asked.

"A while," she said. "But, Norma, what does it matter? An abortion has to be performed in the first twenty-four weeks of pregnancy, and it's clearly too late for you now."

The world stopped.

I've learned this: at horrible, tragic, but also important life-changing moments, there's usually a moment or two of pure truth, total clarity, before the pain and anger flood in.

I had a moment like that right then. I suddenly realized: This lawsuit was not really for me. It was about me, and maybe all the women who'd come before me, but it was really for all the women who were coming after me.

I looked at Linda, who was looking at me sorrowfully. I supposed I'd always known I was too late. I supposed she'd always known it, also. I supposed everyone had known it. I would have to have my baby after all.

There's only one good thing I can say about my anger: it is so strong, so controlling, that in the worst of times—real emergencies—it pushes me right past my worst fears. While it lasts, while I burn inside, it keeps me out of the black holes, the suffocating clouds of hopelessness, waiting to trap me. With anger, I can keep going. For a little while longer, anyway.

That was probably why my third child, the *Roe* baby, made it into this world to be born.

By the time I left Linda's law office I was burning. I was furious at Sarah and Linda. Hadn't they done this to me? Hadn't they led me on, let me think that I could get an abortion—and then, when everything was going fine for them, when they had got what they wanted—they just said, "Sorry," as they told me my world had fallen in?

And now the worst thing I feared had come to pass. This baby, which I had no way to support, was still moving inside me.

I was nothing to Sarah and Linda, nothing more than just a name on a piece of paper. And without them, without their damn legal abortion, my soul was trapped and my body was in jail. I was hopeless. Worthless.

All I had, really, was my anger. My old anger at myself. And my brand-new anger at these two women.

In my anger, I imagined—no, I knew!—that Sarah Weddington and Linda Coffee and all their damn friends were so rich and smart and socially advantaged that just by thinking about it they could arrange an abortion for themselves, or win a court case, or do anything else they damn pleased.

Damn them all to hell, I thought. I would keep going just to spite them. It was the only reason I could think of.

Maybe I had even gone past anger. Maybe I was insane. I cried angry tears and cursed Sarah and Linda's names. I went back to the crash pad, grabbed my duffle bag of clothes and two jugs of wine, and hitchhiked back to my father's house. I found the spare key, under the rock where he kept it, and let myself in. I lay down on the couch, drank my wine, and cried myself to sleep.

The next morning I woke up and made my dad breakfast. I told him that I was broke and out of work and would need his help getting through this pregnancy.

"Sure, Norma," he said, his eyes sad. He told me that of course he would help. He was always there for me. He said he could spare me ten dollars a week in spending money.

In a couple of days I went out looking for work. It was hopeless. No restaurant would hire a waitress who was seven months pregnant. They wouldn't even give me a reason. Why did they need to? They just stared at my stomach and told me to check back with them in a few months. After each rejection I came home, got drunk, and pounded my fists into my belly in frustration.

I called Henry McCluskey. Henry said that he'd talked to Sarah and Linda. He said he was sorry the way things had turned out, that he was worried about me, and that he was glad to hear from me. I spilled out my anger about Sarah, Linda, my mother, my ex-girlfriends, and whoever I else I could think of who had dropped everything and devoted the rest of their lives to ruining mine.

Henry listened to me patiently, and when my rantings and ravings ran down he told me that he'd found a young couple who'd been trying to have their own child for five years. A happily married man and woman were willing to—no, they were excited about—adopting my baby right after it was born. I cursed him and hung up.

He called back. He told me that the couple would pay all my hospital expenses, and maybe even $25 or $50 a week to get me there. I told him to do the paperwork, to get it all arranged, but not to bother me with the details. I didn't want to think about it until I had to.

By my ninth month, my stomach was huge. Bigger than it had ever been. My ankles were so swollen I could barely walk. Maybe, I thought, it was all the beer I was drinking. Maybe it was just the anger filling my body. Maybe it was my worst nightmare, getting ready to happen.

My water broke in the middle of the night. I woke up and walked to the bathroom. I looked down and saw blood pouring out of me. The fluid looked totally different from what had come out the other times. I was terrified. Was the baby dying? Was I dying? I felt as though my whole body was being drained of life.

Frantically, I cleaned myself up as best I could. Then I woke my dad. He got up, got dressed, and helped me outside and into his panel truck, an old clunker with a bad carburetor. It was hard to start, and this time was no exception. Finally, the engine caught and we chugged slowly, very slowly, through the deserted streets.

We got to the hospital, and followed the signs that said EMER-GENCY ROOM around to the back. My father dropped me off at what looked like the emergency room door. I pulled at the door handle. It was locked. I knocked on it. There was no answer. I looked around for a doorbell. I found one and pushed it, but nothing happened.

I slumped down. I didn't know what else to do. I began to have huge cramps, by far the worst I'd ever felt. The pain was horrible, and my clothes were soaking wet.

My father came back and helped me stand up.

"Daddy, I can't walk. You're going to have to go around to the front of the hospital and tell them I'm here."

"No, honey," said my father, "I'm not going to leave you here alone."

Another wave of pain gripped my entire body, like a fist clench-
ing up. I felt like I was going to throw up. There was a glass window, crisscrossed with wires, in the door. When I looked through it
I could see a nurse walking around inside. I stuck my face to the
glass, pounded on the door, and shouted as loud as could that I
was having a baby. That I needed help. That I was dying.

The nurse looked at me, stared, and walked away. I slumped
down again. I could feel the baby coming out of my body. The baby
was being born. And I was bleeding to death.

It finally hit my father what was happening. Maybe he hadn't
really been totally awake until that moment. He swore and
marched around to the front. I lay there in a pool of blood for
what seemed to be hours.

Maybe it was five minutes.

The door to the loading dock opened and the nurse was
there, along with a gurney and a couple of orderlies. They
brought me inside and through the corridor to the real emergency room. The nurse took my name, and I told her to contact
Henry about the adoption. Other hospital people prepped me,
and took me to the delivery room, and the baby was born almost
immediately. Just like the time before, they took the baby away
before I could see it. They wheeled me out and put me to bed
and I fell asleep, exhausted.

I woke up in another room, facing another direction entirely. It
was daytime. A nurse came in. She had so much makeup on that it
looked as if she were wearing a clown mask.

"Time for your shot!" she announced.

"What for?" I said.

"To dry up your breast milk. You're adopting out your baby,
right? So of course you won't be needing it." She left.

After awhile, another woman came in.

"Hello, who are you?" I asked.

"I'm from Administration," she said. "You know, Mrs. McCorvey,
you and I are going to have to have a little talk sometime."

"About what?"

She frowned. Did she think that I was being smart with her?
"Why, about your bill, of course!" she said.

I told her who was taking care of the bill. And also what she could do with it. She left.

Another few hours. Another nurse. This one had a bundled-up baby in her arms.

"Feeding time!" she said.

"What?"

"Feeding time!" she said, again. Then she handed me the baby.

I can't tell you all the horrible feelings that went through me at that moment. It was like getting a glimpse of hell—all my shame and fear and guilt and love and sadness all rolled up into a ball and placed in front of me.

Was this my baby? Why were they giving it to me? Should I look at it? Or not look at it?

I was too full of pain to say anything. Through the blanket, I could feel the baby moving. Breathing.

There was a flap of cloth over its face. My entire body, my entire soul cried out to me to turn the flap down, to look at my baby's face. But my mind told me that it would be worst thing I could ever do.

My mind won. My heart lost. I never touched the flap. I felt sick to my stomach. I started crying, loudly, in pure despair.

The nurse must have seen the expression on my face, because she quickly realized she'd done something awful and ran out of the room. I was left alone with the baby, paralyzed, for another minute or two.

The nurse rushed back in, this time with two orderlies. She pulled the baby out of my arms and handed it to an orderly, who left. Then the baby was gone forever. The nurse didn't say anything to me. She looked scared. She turned to the orderly, who was still standing next to her, and pointed at me.

"You can watch her for me, can't you?" she said to him. He nodded.

"Get out!" I cried, with all the strength I could manage. They both turned and walked out and left me alone. Then I turned my face to the wall and wept.

I wasn't crying when I got home, though. Something inside me told me that I shouldn't. Or didn't even deserve to.

After what had happened to me at the hospital, I was beyond

crying. I was too depressed. The only time I wasn't depressed was when I was drunk.

I got drunk my first night in my father's apartment. I got drunk the next night, and the next. And before long, as soon as I was thin enough to get into my clothes—which was very soon, because I hardly ever felt like eating—I was going out to the bars and getting drunk every night.

Getting drunk at night was no problem. The problem was with the daylight. In the daytime, waking up in my father's house or somewhere else, things were as different as they could be.

I was alone. No, not alone. All my problems—alive and real, like monsters, with faces as ugly and evil as I felt— gathered around to explain to me how I was a failure, an absolute nothing, a piece of garbage, and convince me to give up and stop even trying to be a human being.

I tried to fight the monsters off, to yell back at them, as best I could. But day after day, their arguments got more and more convincing. The fights became longer and longer. It was harder to make them go. I tried to escape them by sleeping, by crying, by walking the streets, by drinking. But they always came back. All of them. Scaring me when they told me who I was, and then when they told me what I had to do. After awhile, I was too tired to fight them. And they knew that.

"We know the truth," they said to me. "And the truth is, Norma, you know the truth, too."

And the truth is, Norma, you know the truth, too.

In my head, I heard them say it even when the demons were gone. And one day, looking into my father's hall mirror, I did know the truth. They didn't have to tell me anymore.

I was bad. Stupid. Hopeless. Queer. A person who should never have been born, who should have given in to the obvious a long time ago.

There it was. Finally. The answer. Yes. All the demons were gone, back deep inside me, and all I was left facing was the truth.

In the stillness and quiet, what I was supposed to do next was obvious. As obvious to me as anything had ever been.

I got out of bed, got dressed. I gathered up all my money, plus all the loose bills and change I could find in the house, and went outside to find the neighborhood drug dealers. When I did, I bought every kind of pill they had. Uppers, downers, speed, Seconal. Pills in all the colors of the rainbow. Pills I'd never even heard of. Pills that even I had been afraid of taking.

By late afternoon I had dozens of pills. I put them in my favorite purse, a little cloth sack that closed at the top like a hobo's pouch.

I put the purse aside and made dinner for my father. That night I didn't go out. That surprised him a little. I lay awake in my bed until early the next morning, waiting for him to go to work.

I got up and tried to decide the best way to kill myself. One that would do the job but wouldn't make me look too bad when people found me. That way I would be remembered as a normal person, not a freak. And I didn't want to cause my father any more trouble than was absolutely necessary. The damn thing, though, was that I couldn't decide what to do. My brain was slowing down, refusing to work. I couldn't think. It was aggravating.

I took all the pills out of my purse, lined them up on the dining room table, and stared at them. Get moving, Norma, they said to me. Don't try to fool us. You know what to do.

I took a handful of pills and swallowed them. Then I got up and got dressed. I chose my favorite T-shirt. You had to look closely to figure it out, but in fancy psychedelic writing it said, "*Fuck You.*"

This will be a good final statement to make, I thought. I looked into my bag to see if I'd gotten all the pills, and found a five-dollar bill scrunched into the bottom. Fantastic! I thought. Everything was falling into place.

I ironed my best pair of bluejeans and put them on. I put on my makeup.

I took the five dollars and went to the beer store and bought a bottle of Wild Turkey. It cost $5.98, but the man said that it would be no trouble if I owed him the rest and came back later with it.

On the way home I cracked open the bottle and took my first sip. Yes! That was what I was going to do. That was my plan. I'd take some pills, then swallow some liquor, and when I felt myself going I would walk over to the living room couch and lie down. That would be how people would find me. Lying on the couch. Peaceful. Saying fuck you to the world: "Fuck you, world!"

There were exactly thirty-two steps from my dad's dining room table to the couch. I counted them each time I made the trip. I told myself: I'll take five or six pills every ten minutes. Then I'll lie on the couch to see if I've taken enough.

Pills. Couch. Pills. Couch. Liquor. When I couldn't feel anything happening, I changed the pill-taking to every five minutes.

Just as I began to run out of pills, I began to hallucinate. I hadn't planned on hallucinating. The pills that were left were getting up and doing some pretty weird things, like waving to me, and spinning around, and flipping over backwards. I was totally amused at what I was seeing. The pills were all different colors, different sizes, different shapes, and they were all getting up and performing. They were performing for me.

They were showing me how cute they were. How talented they were. And I wished I were cute, I wished I were talented. I wished I knew what that woman down the hall knew. And I knew that these pills were smarter than I am, because look at what they're doing.

Then I think I lost consciousness at the table. I dreamed that my body was in a well, and there was just enough room for me to put my knees up against one wall and lean back on the other wall. Because the well was circular.

I heard someone call my name. I was conscious again, or in another dream, because I was sitting in my chair and hearing someone call my name and I was looking out the window for them. I looked very hard. I could see this person's shadow on the window, but it seemed like the closer I'd get to the window, the more they'd go away.

All of the sudden the shadow was gone, the presence was gone, and I knew, right then, that I was dying. Because I remembered all the stories I'd read when I was a kid, about how you see the light at the end of the tunnel, you know, and how your whole life flashes before your eyes.

Now it was pitch dark in my dad's apartment. I was feeling very lightweight. As if I'd lost gravity. And I kept thinking about how disgusting my life had been. How unfair. How this would really show them. How this would really hurt people. How when they come in here and they find my body and realize that I'm dead, it's really going to hurt them.

I'll be free. I'll be free from worry, I'll be free from loving, I'll be free from pain. I will no longer be.

I enjoyed feeling that inner peace. But then the next thing I knew I was in my dad's bedroom. And I was alive. If I were dead, I wouldn't be lying in his bed. My eyes wouldn't be open. And I wouldn't see him sitting next to me.

✑ 12 ✑

As you can see from the preceding chapters, I didn't have much to do with the actual battle for *Roe* v. *Wade*. While I was having my baby and crushing myself under my own despair, *Roe* v. *Wade* was moving forward without me. In fact, after I stormed out of their office, I didn't talk to Sarah or Linda until nearly a year after the *Roe* baby was born. None of this really mattered in the legal world, though.

In legal terms, what Sarah and Linda did was miraculous. Using me as their plaintiff, they successfully challenged the Texas state law forbidding abortions. And they won, even though the decision came too late for me to abort.

Before the trial, Sarah and Linda had worried about this. To guard against the court throwing out our case, they had added a "class action" to the lawsuit, stating that it was now being fought on behalf not only of me but on behalf of all the unnamed American women everywhere who were or would be in my situation.

Interestingly, Sarah and Linda didn't tell me they'd done the class action. They also never mentioned that *Roe* v. *Wade* was the first court case that either one of them had ever tried.

At the state trial, Sarah and Linda argued that the law against abortion was too vague—that abortion couldn't be "murder," as the anti-abortionists called it, because nobody really knew if, or more important, when a fetus was considered a person under the law. They also argued that the anti-abortion law violated the Ninth Amendment to the Constitution, which guarantees Americans the right to privacy and their own decisions, including the important one of whether or not they wanted to have children.

All three judges bought their arguments. They declared the Texas anti-abortion law unconstitutional.

Unfortunately, all that meant was that Sarah and Linda and their supporters had won the first round. After the decision, Henry Wade immediately announced that until all his appeals were exhausted he would still prosecute doctors who did abortions. Because of that, no doctor in Texas was willing to do abortions, and therefore no Texas woman was able to get one.

Pro-choice Texans would have to keep fighting Henry Wade and the anti-abortionists in the higher courts. For Sarah, especially, the decision to keep fighting was automatic.

In the summer of 1970, she and her husband moved to Fort Worth. Sarah got a job as an assistant district attorney, and Ron Weddington, who had just graduated from law school, began work in private practice. In the fall, with the help of Roy Lucas, a New York lawyer who worked for an organization that specialized in women's cases, they filed papers with the U.S. Supreme Court asking that *Roe* v. *Wade* be heard in the highest court immediately. Sarah and her friends also campaigned to pass a bill in the Texas legislature to make abortion legal.

The bill lost. But in Washington, the Supreme Court justices were aware that abortion was one of the most important and controversial issues in America, and that several successful challenges to state abortion laws were being appealed. In March 1971 the judges announced that *Roe* v. *Wade* would be heard in front of the Supreme Court. Along with a Georgia case, *Doe* v. *Bolton*, it would represent all similar pro-choice lawsuits from all over the country. In other words, our case would help decide whether the U.S. Constitution guaranteed that American women had the right to have babies—or terminate their pregnancies—as they chose.

Sarah quit her district attorney job and moved to Austin with Ron to open their own practice. Then she moved temporarily to New York City, where she prepared her Supreme Court argument with the help of Roy Lucas's organization. The work was complicated and exhausting, and Sarah and Roy Lucas were not compatible partners. As the hearing date got closer, Sarah writes in her book, the work was not getting done.

A little bit of panic set in. Ron Weddington shut down the Austin practice and flew east to help his wife. Sarah and Lucas clashed seriously: they each wanted to be the lawyer arguing the actual case in front of the Supreme Court. To solve her problem, Sarah got in touch with me, for the first time in a long time.

On December 13, 1971, in Washington, D.C., Sarah argued the case before Justices Harry Blackmun, William Brennan, Warren Burger, William Douglas, Thurgood Marshall, Potter Stewart, and Byron White. Two seats on the Court were empty at this time. Sarah was twenty-seven years old. She spoke for thirty minutes, presenting much the same arguments about the beginning of life and the Ninth Amendment that she had made back in Austin. A lawyer named Jay Floyd, representing Texas and Henry Wade, also repeated his earlier arguments in opposing her.

The judges adjourned. Their decision would come in a few months.

Sarah and Ron went back to Austin. While they waited for the decision, Sarah decided to start a new career as a politician. She ran for an Austin seat in the Texas House of Representatives. Ron and many of her college and law school friends were active in her campaign. A lawyer's wife named Ann Richards—now governor of Texas—was one of her chief campaign volunteers.

Among Austin Democrats, Sarah's position on the abortion question gained her political support. In early June she won a primary election to gain the Democratic nomination. On June 26, the U.S. Supreme Court made its announcement on *Roe* v. *Wade:* the judges wanted the case reargued in front of them.

This was a rare request for the Supreme Court, and its reasons for making it have never been fully explained. Some experts think that the court wanted the full number of nine justices to hear this important case.

Whatever the reason, it meant that Sarah had to take a break from her campaign, travel to Washington, D.C., and reargue *Roe.* On October 11, 1972, three weeks before she won her Texas House seat in a landslide, Sarah stood up before justices Blackmun,

Brennan, Burger, Douglas, Marshall, Lewis Powell, William Rehnquist, Stewart, and White. She stated the same deeply held ideas, then went home to begin her new career. The final decision would come shortly.

As for me, Jane Roe, I had no idea that the verdict was coming. I learned about it just like everyone else.

⮂ 13 ⮀

Iwoke up from my suicide attempt in my father's bed. To this day, I don't know how I got there.

When I came to, the first thought in my mind was that I was still alive. My second thought was what my still being alive meant—that I hadn't managed to kill myself. That I'd failed as badly at ending my life as I had at everything else I'd ever tried to do. And now I was stuck here: doomed to live out my life as long as anyone else.

That thought, that second, was terrifying.

I thought I was alone. But out of the corner of my eye, I saw a movement, which became a face. It was my father's face, looking as worried as I'd ever seen it. He was bending over me.

Shouldn't he be at work? He never stays home from work. . . . And then I couldn't think about that anymore, because I was sick. I turned my head to the side and gagged. My father reached down and put a kitchen bowl in front of my face. I leaned over the side of the bed, bringing up all the pills and poisons until my stomach was empty. Then my father helped me sit up.

"Daddy, what are you doing home?" I said.

"Well, hell, girl," he said, "you're finally waking up. You know, I found you passed out, dead to the world, when I came home yesterday. And now it's the middle of the next damn afternoon."

I wanted to clamp my arms around him and tell him how scared I was of living. How painful it all was to me. And what I had tried to do to put an end to it, once and for all.

But for some reason, I couldn't move. My arms were stuck to my sides.

"The middle of the afternoon!" said my father. He shook his head and forced a grin.

"You know," he said, "there's one damn thing that I never taught any of my kids, and that was how to drink.

"Girl, you must have pulled a really good drunk last night. You drank a whole damn quart of Wild Turkey. You didn't really want to do that, do you?"

"No, Daddy. I didn't."

"All right, then. Good," he said.

He lifted me out of his bed and put me in my own. I was very tired, falling back to sleep. Maybe a few of those pills, I thought, were still rattling around inside me. But as I fell asleep, the last thing I thought was: my father actually stayed home from work to watch over me.

I still couldn't believe it.

When I woke up the next time it was the middle of the night, and my father was asleep. I sat up in my bed and cried.

I cried until morning, out of frustration and fear and the pain of knowing that somebody, somewhere, for some reason—who was it? was it God? my mother? the Devil?—would never let me resolve things, make them come out even close to the way I wanted them to.

I knew I was a bad person. A complete failure. And that my curse was to walk the earth, banging my head against every wall I needed to get over, trying to find a safe place, a little crack where I could fit in, a little bit of peace—even if, for me, there was no such thing.

But there was no other way out. I had no choice.

All I knew was what I already knew. All I could do was what I could do. When morning came, I got up and made breakfast for my dad. Then I got dressed and went on living my life.

Most days—though not that day, and not on many other bad days that were to come in the future—I'm glad I did.

Looking back at my suicide attempt, I realize that this low point was really a turning point. Somewhere, pushed very deep down, the real reasons for continuing to live were already inside me.

These reasons were, I think, that in my twisted, self-defeating way, I had a lot of pushed-down feelings of love to express that were struggling to get out. And that no matter how much of a failure I felt, I really did make some sort of difference in the world—with some people, somewhere.

That was what *Roe* v. *Wade* was mostly about, after all. But back then Jane Roe, whoever she was, couldn't help Norma McCorvey. Norma McCorvey was a lonely, depressed woman, who needed to get through the next day and the next. And as each new day began, she didn't have a clue about how to do it again.

Each new day brought a different problem. And, sometimes, a little glimpse of hope.

When I was able to go out again, I headed straight for the bars, of course. But this time I got lucky. I got to talking with Caroline,[*] a service station owner with two children. She told me that her lover, Judith,[*] had been a college student before taking a dose of bad acid that had ruined her mind. Now Judith stayed at Caroline's house. Caroline was looking for someone to take care of her during the day. She had a little money to pay that person. I told her that the job was probably something I could do.

It was probably the best thing I could have done. Taking care of Judith helped me forget my own problems, if just for a little while. From seven A.M. to three P.M., while Caroline ran the station and her son and daughter were in school, I stayed home with Judith. It was obvious immediately that her bad acid trip had kept on after the drug wore off. I couldn't lead her back to the real world, but I did my best. I cooked her her meals, helped her get dressed and cleaned up, and talked to her about whatever was on my mind.

Most of the time Judith sat quietly, lost inside herself, gone to places no one could understand. But other times she needed to be rescued. She would strip off her clothes and stand in the shower, scrubbing herself, the water turned off. She would fly into violent rages, fits of screaming and cursing and kicking and hitting herself that scared even me—especially when it made me think about my own anger. To calm her down I'd hold on to her tightly and talk to her as soothingly as I could. Eventually, we could rock together into silence.

Then there were times when Judith sounded almost normal, like the smart college student she used to be. Or she'd become a little girl of six. Or three.

One day she left the house when I wasn't looking. I don't know how she did it, Caroline and I kept the doors locked from the both inside and outside all the time.

I was frantic. I thought I had lost her. I was certain she'd be killed, or kidnapped and raped, and it would be my fault forever.

I ran around the neighborhood, looking for her, and finally found her in her own backyard, standing quietly and looking at the trees. She was calm and happy to see me. She wanted to show me what she had discovered. She pointed out the bats flying from one tree to another. Only she could see them.

Every weekday, after Caroline got home from work, I would say good-bye to Judith, go over to one bar or another, and drink myself into forgetfulness. I kept this up for six months. After six months, I realized I just couldn't keep on doing it. The nights spent in the bars weren't helping me face Judith—or myself—the next morning. I didn't have enough patience for both Judith and me. My own restlessness was breaking through.

Caroline said she understood. She hadn't been able to pay me much, after all. So after a few weeks looking for a job—occasionally getting a shift or two working behind a bar—I was once again at the ragged edge, living on what my father could spare me.

He couldn't spare me much, the poor man. One day, broke and hungry and angry, I stole some food from a convenience store—and for once, my weakness and stupidity didn't bring me pain. It was just the opposite, actually. At this low point in my life, a crime I committed bought me love and companionship. It brought me the woman who's been the most important person in my life for seventeen years.

Who knows why it happened that way? Maybe we all get one or two of these free chances in life. As usual, I did my best to waste it.

The store was on the edge of a Mexican neighborhood, and it was tiny—just barely big enough to turn around in. The only

employee, the manager, was a woman—and she was on the telephone, her back to me as I came in. There was no way, I figured,
that she could see me as I wandered through the aisles.

It was the middle of the afternoon, and I hadn't eaten since
breakfast. I walked around, looking things over. I grabbed some
crackers, a can of soup, and two cans of Coke. I stuffed them under
my blouse. I lifted a few other items and put them into my purse. I
sneaked a peak at the woman up front. Still on the phone. Still
with her back to me. No way I was going to get caught. I made my
way past the checkout stand and halfway to the front door. Home
free. The street was just a few steps away.

"You know," said a voice behind me, "I really should call the
cops on you."

Damn.

I whirled around and saw the manager, dark and short-haired
and a little stocky, standing and looking at me with her hands on
her hips. She was grinning at me, damn her.

"Well, hell," I said, "do you want me to give you the damn
phone number?"

Her grinning at me like that, as if it was the funniest thing in
the world that she'd caught me, made me mad.

"Oh, Miss Toughie!" she laughed. She had brown eyes, and
they were laughing, too.

"No, just hungry," I said.

From under my blouse I pulled out the things I'd stolen and
showed them to her.

"Here, take the damn things," I said.

She laughed again and waved me out. I was shocked. It was the
nicest thing any stranger had done for me in a long time.

I went home and ate. The next day I came back and offered to
work for her—I told her I'd sweep floors or do anything else she
needed—until I'd paid her back for the food I'd stolen. She smiled
and said she'd think it over. Then she told me to stand in back of
the counter until she finished her shift.

"Yeah, okay. Right," I said.

Behind the counter I found out her secret: there was a hubcap-
shaped mirror above the cash register. When she looked into it she
could see over her shoulder to every part of the damn store.

In fact, I could see her in the aisle—looking at me looking into the mirror. Looking at her. "Well, hell," she said, in a make-believe gruff voice, "I can't let you steal me blind now, can I, girl?" Then she took off her apron, brought me outside, and showed me her car. It was a cherry red '69 Plymouth, with bucket seats and four on the floor. She opened the door for me on the passenger side, and then she drove me home.

"See you around, girl," she said to me. She told me later that she'd fallen in love with me that very first day.

Within a few weeks, I was living with this woman. Her name was Connie Gonzales. And I didn't love her. Not yet.

But learning to love her, which didn't happen overnight, was maybe the finest thing I've ever done.

Connie Gonzales was in her middle thirties when she entered my life. She is half-Mexican and half-Italian. She was born in Chicago, and after her parents broke up when she was a baby, lived there with her father. At eighteen, she left home and went to Texas to find her mother. She and her mom fell into each other's arms, but her stepbrother and stepsisters ostracized her when they found out she was a lesbian.

That was terrible and cruel of them, and it tears her up inside to this day. But the truth is, Connie could no more keep herself in the closet than walk on the moon. Connie has known she is a lesbian all her life. And that is fine with her. She loves women. She would no more want to change that part of her than change her name, or her handsome face, or her strong hands.

Connie has worked hard at many kinds of jobs, sometimes alongside women, sometimes as the only woman alongside men, nearly all her life. She has been an air-conditioning repairperson, a construction worker, and a machinist. Now she works in a factory, making engine parts. She has lived in the same house for nearly twenty-five years. I've lived there with her for seventeen of them. A few years ago, like any other old married couple, we finally paid off the mortgage and celebrated.

Since we've known each other, Connie has taken care of me in hundreds of ways. I have taken care of her as best I can. Emotionally, she is as different from me as night from day. On the outside, she is calm, confident, and peaceful. On the inside, she worries. Almost all the time.

It's hard to say, exactly, when the moment was that we became a couple. On the very day that she drove me home in her Plymouth, she called me at my father's house and asked me to go out to dinner with her. I told her I was too busy and too poor to have a girlfriend. That I had to find a job. So she called me up again and again. And I turned her down again and again, until I realized that fighting somebody so calm and patient and in love with me would be useless.

I went out with her. And when she invited me to a party at her house and told me to pack an overnight bag, I yelled at her for being presumptuous. Then I packed my bag and came over. On another day soon after that she told me to pack all my clothes, that I was moving in with her. When I finally agreed to go with her, she drove over to my dad's place to help me pack up my things. Then she took my father out to the parking lot, by herself, and promised him that she would take care of me for the rest of my life. That she would never knowingly let anyone else harm me or hurt me.

My father told Connie that he was happy to hear her say that. And whatever has happened between her and me since then, she has never broken her promise.

Connie Gonzales's house was in the suburbs, far from the bars and busy streets where I'd spent so much of my life. Living without the noise and the one-night stands and the late hours and the beer and the liquor, I had more time on my hands than I'd had in years. To my surprise, the empty hours didn't make me nervous. I had more energy, and I had clear-headedness, too.

I was ready to go back to work. The owner of the store where Connie worked had decided to fire her and work the counter himself. So I had a good idea. Maybe the best one in years. Sitting on the front porch, looking out on our little street, I decided that Connie and I would start a business.

We would be our own bosses, free from anyone hiring us or firing us or telling us how we could run our lives.

What could we do? The answer came surprisingly easily. We would clean apartments. Have our own cleaning service. Do the dirty work that nobody else wanted to do. And the plan worked. *We* worked.

Connie and I worked as hard as we've ever worked in our lives. So hard that sometimes our problems and past lives almost faded into forgetfulness.

We called our little business N. L. McCorvey & Company. At least, that was the name on our stationery—when I remembered, after months of rubber stamps and stationery store forms and writing on the backs of envelopes, to order some.

In the beginning, all we had was a phone book. I turned the yellow pages to APARTMENT BUILDINGS and called all over the Dallas–Fort Worth area to every manager or landlord I could get hold of. I then offered to clean two apartments free of charge. If they liked our service, they could hire us to clean up the messes left by negligent or evicted tenants. They could pay us with their ex-tenants' security deposits.

Our price was right. Lots of people wanted to try us out. It was while I was making up our schedule one day that the phone rang and I picked it up, expecting to hear from a new customer. Instead, it was Sarah Weddington.

I was surprised to hear her voice, to say the least. I honestly didn't think she would ever need to talk to me again. But she'd gone to the trouble of getting in touch with my father and managed, without telling him I was Jane Roe, to get him to give her Connie's number.

The reason she was calling, said Sarah, was legal. As she explained it to me she seemed to think she was making crystal-clear sense, but all I could figure out was that there seemed to be some complicated lawyers' battle over who should represent me in the next part, an important part, of *Roe* v. *Wade*.

As far as I could make out, I had to solve this for her. Sarah sounded anxious—and when she was anxious she always used complicated words. Moving these words around, putting them in different order, Sarah tried a few times to explain what she meant. Finally, I began to figure out that the job of representing me was up for grabs between Sarah and some man in New York.

"Some man in New York I've never met?"

"Yes," Sarah said.

"Well, sure. You do it, Sarah," I said.

"Thank you, Norma," said Sarah.

Already, even as we were speaking, I was getting nervous and upset. I was glad there wasn't anything more, really, to discuss. Sarah thanked me again for choosing her and hung up.

N. L. McCorvey & Company charged $25 per apartment, cleaned from top to bottom. Most of our customers' buildings were in bad neighborhoods. Many of the places we entered hadn't been cleaned in a long, long time. If ever. More than a few had either been lived in by lunatics or animals, or deliberately trashed.

At five o'clock each morning, Connie and I would load up with mops and brooms and Lysol and Comet and paper towels, ride together to the day's job, and split up until we were finished.

We usually weren't finished until dark. We'd tackle the bathrooms—the worst part—first. Then the kitchens, making sure to move all the appliances. Then the carpets, the venetian blinds, the insides of the windows, and the closets.

More often than not, the last tenant—or somebody, some poor anybody—had left clothes or shoes or bedclothes, forgotten, in the closets. They were long gone, so it was part of our deal that we got to keep everything we came across. On the weekends we held garage sales to add a little extra money per hour.

When we got home each night, we would be so covered with dirt and filth that first Connie, then I, would stand on our front porch and slip out of our disgusting coveralls, drop them in a heap, and run as fast as we could to the shower—being careful not to touch anything in the house on our way.

After a few months of trial cleaning jobs—of showing up when we said we would and charging the same price we quoted over the phone—the landlords decided that Connie and I were legitimate. They began asking us back. They began asking us if we could paint their empty apartments, also.

We said yes, even though neither of us knew how to use a paintbrush. We taught ourselves, practicing at home on our own walls, and then we charged $45 per paint job. Neither us knew much about bookkeeping. But after a year or so, it wasn't such a strain to buy supplies or new sneakers or do a whole week's worth of grocery shopping in one trip to feel we were making progress.

I distinctly remember one special moment: deciding that we had enough money in the bank to risk paying a month in advance to have the newspaper delivered.

That was why, on the afternoon I came home with $200 in my pocket—payment for a week's worth of painting jobs—the *Times-Herald* was waiting for us.

While Connie took her shower, I sat at the kitchen table, drinking a beer and reading. The big news that day was that Lyndon Johnson had died. There was a big headline, and articles on the front page about his life and the Vietnam War and what LBJ meant for the state of Texas. I kept reading.

My eyes wandered to the lower right-hand corner of the page. There was a small, matter-of-fact article that said that the United States Supreme Court had legalized abortion all over the United States. That it was now perfectly okay for a woman to get an abortion in Texas, or anywhere else. That the court had decided seven to two in favor of an anonymous plaintiff in a test case, a challenge to the anti-abortion law, called *Roe* v. *Wade.*

The article talked about the attorneys in the case. It talked about the Supreme Court justices. Which ones voted for it, which ones against it. But it didn't have anything to say about the plaintiff.

The *plaintiff.* I knew what the word meant now. I knew how to spell it and I knew what it was like to be one. And I knew the plaintiff. I knew all about her. I knew what it meant to want an abortion and not be able to have one.

For a long while I just stared into space, fighting my emotions.

"What's wrong, honey?" said Connie, coming in all cleaned up and seeing me just sitting there.

"They've legalized abortion," I told her, handing her the paper.

"Oh. Okay. That's good," she said, reading.

After a few seconds, I interrupted her.

"Connie. Do you see where they mention the plaintiff? A woman called Jane Roe?"

"Yeah. Sure I do," said Connie, looking puzzled.

I looked her straight in the eye and said: "How would you like to meet Jane Roe?"

Connie laughed. But when she saw I was serious, she looked at me and laughed softly.

"Oh, Pixie, come on," said Connie. "We don't know anybody like that."

∾ 14 ∾

Sarah Weddington and Linda Coffee had done it. With the help of the hundreds of people who supported them, they had won their case, made history, and greatly improved the lives of American women, rich and poor.

The 1973 decision on *Roe* v. *Wade* declared that all state anti-abortion laws, like the one in Texas that completely prohibited abortion, were absolutely unconstitutional. *Doe* v. *Bolton*, which was decided favorably at the same time as our case, wiped out all the abortion "reform" laws—the laws that, in certain states, had put limited abortion rights in the hands of doctors and hospital committees or had insisted that only state residents be allowed to get abortions in their states.

Most of the judges of the Supreme Court had agreed with Sarah's arguments and voted, by a wide margin, to legalize abortion. Voting for *Roe* were justices Blackmun, Brennan, Burger, Douglas, Marshall, Powell, and Stewart. Voting for *Wade* were justices Rehnquist and White.

The judges ruled, just as Sarah had written, that anti-abortion laws violated the Fourteenth Amendment—the one that guaranteed "life, liberty, and property." Anti-abortion laws did this, agreed the judges, by violating a woman's right to privately control her own body.

They ruled that the opposite argument—that a fetus was a separate human being entitled to legal protection—was not backed up by anything in the Constitution.

The judges did say, though, that states might outlaw abortions after the point where a fetus had "the capability of meaningful life" if it left the mother's womb. What this meant was that abortions after the second trimester could be outlawed.

Roe v. *Wade* determined that any pregnant woman—even a poor, noneducated woman—could decide whether or not she was going to continue with her pregnancy. She could happily choose to bear the child, give birth to it, love it, and raise it; or, if for some reason she felt she was unable to accept that tremendous responsibility, she could get an abortion without asking anyone's permission.

It was, of course, too late for me. But after the *Roe* decision came down, thousands of women took advantage of their new freedom. Abortions became a normal medical procedure: at first in hospitals, soon afterwards in newly formed abortion clinics. Many of these clinics were run by the same brave doctors who had risked their livelihoods by preforming illegal abortions pre-*Roe*.

For $150 or $200, anyone could obtain a legal, safe, doctor-supervised abortion. The procedure, especially in the first months of pregnancy, was quick and private. It was nobody's business but that of the woman involved.

Poor women choosing to abort could have their bill paid, just as for any other medical procedure, by state Medicaid plans. The back-alley abortionists and butcher shops and abortion gangsters were immediately put out of business. It was the beginning of a glorious era of women's reproductive freedom and happiness. It lasted for only a little while. Then the fight began all over again.

∽ 15 ∽

Unlike me, Connie Gonzalez is a kind, open-hearted, forgiving person. That she and I love each other very much, and always will, is a great gift, which I will always feel I do not deserve. That she believed me instantly when I told her I was Jane Roe is just one mark of our trust and faith in each other. That she still loved me, even after she found I'd been hiding a big part of my life from her, was another.

The night I found out that *Roe* v. *Wade* had been decided I cried. Eventually I drank myself to sleep.

The next morning we went to work. Connie didn't ask me a question all day. When we came home that evening, though, she asked me if I was feeling ready to talk about it. I was.

Over the living room table I told Connie everything. I told her how I become Jane Roe. I told her about my anger and frustration over the case. About my strained relationship with Sarah Weddington and about my biggest fear—that my lie about being raped would somehow be found out and both Jane Roe and I would be exposed as liars.

I told Connie that I was proud of being Jane Roe, even though being found out scared me, now more than ever. Would I go to jail? Would the whole case then be overturned? Would abortion then be illegal again, and would millions of women in America go back to suffering and helplessness?

Just because of my telling a lie?

"Oh, I don't know about that, Pixie," said Connie. But she agreed that staying anonymous might be the best idea for the time being. If I decided to keep my identity secret, well then, my secret was safe with her.

I kissed her and thanked her, and in a few days the abortion story disappeared from the newspaper entirely. There were other stories, other crises, other court cases for everyone in America to worry about.

From the whole world around me, silence. Yet, lying awake at night, I thought about myself and Jane Roe. I realized that she was a big part of me, and that I would probably never get rid of her. She and I would have to come to some sort of agreement eventually. And do things together.

But what were those things? All I knew was that I was scared of them, whatever they were. So I drank most nights to fall asleep and to stop the questions. I went on with my life. But things were just not the same. Not for me, and not for everyone.

One day, there was a women's rights demonstration in downtown Dallas. I'd never heard of or seen anything like that in Dallas before, and one part of me wanted to go down to see what was going on. What was going on, I thought, was something I might be interested in. What I didn't know, and what chilled me to the bone when I saw it on television later, was that the women's rights demonstrators had been jeered, booed, and later even attacked by anti-abortion demonstrators. The police had to be called to break up the screaming mobs. I took a bus—a late one, because another big part of me was scared to show my face—and made it downtown just as the rally was breaking up.

By the time I arrived at the rally site, the only people still there were anti-abortion picketers. They looked angry, intense. I think they were more than a little frustrated at having nobody left to demonstrate against.

One man, holding an anti-abortion sign, cursed the women who had been speaking earlier at the rally, calling them bitches and dykes and man-haters. And worse. A woman standing next to him smiled at him, then said, "That goddamned Jane Roe woman! If I ever catch her, I'll kill her!"

"Damn right," said the man. I felt paralyzed. Sick to my stomach. I began to tremble.

In shock, I turned to her and stammered, "Wh-why? Wh-why do you want to kill her?"

"Because she kills babies."

She looked at me suspiciously. "Don't you know that?"

"Uh, no. I don't know that," I said.

After she scowled at me and walked away, I ran all the way back to the bus stop. I was anonymous, I thought, as I ran. Anonymous—that's who Jane Roe is. Anonymous.

When the bus stopped in our neighborhood I was still trembling. I didn't leave the house for a few days. I tried to stop shaking, and I tried to figure out why that woman had said such a hateful thing to me.

I'd never killed a baby. I'd never even had an abortion. All I'd tried to do was get control of myself, tried to straighten out my life. Yet, this woman wanted to kill me.

Me. And Jane Roe. Both of us, together. Kill one, kill the other.

But underneath the fear, I felt just a tiny spark of a different kind of anger.

I saw a piece on the TV news about a women's health clinic near our house. The woman they interviewed said that the clinic was also a center for women's rights, and that the local campaign for the Equal Rights Amendment was being run out of the same building. She looked friendly, and the things she said, about equal opportunity and higher wages for women's work, made sense to me. I worked up my courage, went over to the clinic, and volunteered my spare time.

The women at the clinic put me to work right away. I stuffed envelopes with flyers, addressed them and mailed them, and phoned women to remind them of meetings. I even made a couple of friends among the volunteers at the center and told them confidentially, just between us, that I was Jane Roe.

They said they were glad to know me. We worked together for a few weeks, until there was an exciting day at the clinic. A major figure in the women's movement, the head of one of its largest and most powerful organizations, had come to visit us.

She walked around the office, standing very tall and sure of herself, shaking hands with everyone.

"Hi, I'm Norma McCorvey," I said to her. And then, for some reason—in order to make more contact with her? or because she looked so cool and confident and together, and I was so intimidated?—I blurted out, "I'm the Jane Roe of *Roe* v. *Wade.*"

She looked at me, smiled, and shook her head. "No, no," she said.

"I know who Jane Roe is. She wouldn't be here doing this kind of work."

She moved on. I put down my work, went home and cried. I didn't go back.

Luckily, I had my own work to do. Before I knew it, Connie and I were living a kind of life that I'd barely even imagined. We worked hard. Very hard. Maybe too hard: in order to get a jump on the rush hour, Connie and I would leave the house at 3 A.M. to start on our first empty apartment of the day. We'd work all day and collapse at home, exhausted, by late afternoon. The economy was bad, so our business was good. Hundreds of people, especially in the poor neighborhoods where we usually worked, were getting evicted every day.

Tenants abandoned their apartments—just left their belongings and disappeared into the night. The landlords called us.

We entered apartments that we were told were empty and found old people, alone or in couples, who had stayed on secretly. Some were confused and didn't understand what was happening to them. Others were just too terrified to leave. If we could, we'd just tell the manager and move on to our next job. Two times we unlocked a front door and found elderly tenants inside dead, from heart attacks. One had been locked up with her cat for two or three days.

We took every job that was offered to us. Once, we cleaned up for the Dallas PD after a double murder. The bodies were gone by the time we arrived, but dried blood was spattered all over the walls and floor and the ceiling.. Two gay men had gotten drunk and slashed themselves with broken wine bottles. Or, at least, that's what the policeman told us.

Very early one morning, in a particularly bad neighborhood,

Connie and I pulled up for a new job and couldn't find the manager, who had arranged to meet us there. We walked around her building, looking for her—until Connie and I saw something that had been a person, floating face down in the middle of the swimming pool.

We ran away and called the police. We later found out that it was the manager, the woman we were looking for. She had been killed somewhere else, the night before, and thrown into the water. They never found her murderer.

Seeing such things was frightening and depressing. But occasionally, when the shock and fear wore off, something else struck me: that for the first time I had a decent job and a family—Connie—and that many of the people I met every day weren't as loved or as well off as I was. I felt bad for them. But I also felt separated a little bit from the pain and suffering and desperation I saw all around me.

Could I have really lived like that, alone and on the edge of a bottomless black pit, for all those years?

I was changing, I realized. Old habits were slipping away. After working for twelve straight hours, I didn't have any energy left to go partying or bar-hopping, even though a part of me, remembering the sweet mindlessness of getting drunk or high every night, missed it bad. There was also a part of me that felt, as we scrubbed and painted and drove the freeways, that I ought to be spending even more time counting our money and phoning for jobs. Planning ahead. And thinking about Melissa.

I thought about Melissa more than ever. My daughter was ten years old now. She was a beautiful little girl, thin and dark-haired and shy. For most of her life, she had lived with her grandmother and her boyfriend, moving back and forth with them between Texas and Louisiana.

I called Missy when I could and visited her when my mother and my circumstances allowed. Now, though, I was ready to become as much of a mother as I possibly could.

It was heartbreaking. Despite everything that had happened, my mother still terrified me and brought out my old wild rage. She cursed me almost every time we talked, calling me a damned queer and a worthless bitch. But there was also something—her age? my home? my steady relationship with Connie?—that allowed both of us, finally, to loosen up just a bit. Probably just as much as we possibly could.

But it wasn't enough.

After Connie and I began living together and my telephone number stayed the same for more than a few weeks at a time, my mother, who was living in the area, began to bring Melissa over occasionally for short visits. These visits lasted as long as we managed to keep our temper.

The few hours we had together were wonderful. And painful and nerve-racking at the same time. I knew Missy knew I was her mother, but I also felt certain my mother had told her terrible things about me. When we talked about her school or her friends, when we played with her dolls together, when I held her, I could feel her pulling back. Withdrawing. Scared.

It didn't help much that when my mother brought Melissa to see me she always dressed her in her best Sunday clothes and told her strictly and firmly not to mess them up. I was told that, too. It seemed like an incredible risk just to make Melissa a sandwich or take her out to play in our backyard. To me, although I tried to fight the feeling, she seemed fragile. Something to be looked at through a pane of glass. Too delicate for the likes of me to touch.

Sometimes, I cried when I saw her.

"Norma, isn't she pretty?" my mother would say, holding my daughter's little hand tightly and walking her back and forth in front of me.

"Yes, Mother," I'd say.

"Isn't she nice? Isn't she well behaved?"

"Yes, Mother."

"Norma, don't you wish you could have been half as nice when you were a little girl?"

After that I would usually say something smart-mouthed to her, and that would start the usual big fight, and we would begin yelling and screaming and Melissa would start crying and that would be the end of the visit. And all future visits, according to my mother, forever.

Except that in a few months the call would come, or one of my calls would be returned, and another visit would be planned. And one time, just that one time, Missy stayed behind with me, and I got a bittersweet look at what could have been.

It's hard for me to remember exactly why my mother arrived out of the blue one afternoon and told me that Missy would be living with Connie and me from now on.

Maybe she had had a fight with Raymond. They broke up and got back together two or three times that I remember. Or maybe, in her fifties, she felt tired of being Melissa's mother and grandmother at the same time. Maybe Mary Mildred just felt restless, in search of new companions.

Whatever the reason, for six months, Melissa, my own sweet daughter, was all mine. I had Connie with me, also. It was a wonderful time.

It was also a very serious time—for all three of us. I knew I had a lot to make up to Melissa. By the time my daughter moved in with us she was a young woman, almost as tall as I was. She had girlfriends I'd never heard of, clothes I'd never bought for her, homework problems that I couldn't really help her with.

Sadly, I couldn't be the young mother she had missed while I was growing up myself. But I swore to do the best I possibly could.

We gave Melissa her own little room, right next to mine. We moved her in there with her toys and her clothes and her bed and her own TV. I signed her up at the local grade school, and I arranged my work schedule so I could walk her there and pick her up every day.

At first, she was as nervous and scared as I was. But I figured that was only natural. After all, I told myself, my mother—the only mother she had ever known—had left her with me, a woman my mother had probably taught her was as evil as the devil.

So I took things slowly. I fought down my impatience, the nervous, sad feeling that I had to push things along to make up for the lost time between us. I wasn't half as strict with her as my mother had been with me. I made sure of that. I cut way down on my drinking. I struggled harder than ever to control my temper. And with my sweet daughter, around, it was easy.

I played with her and cleaned up after her—sometimes, in fact, she did the same for me. I bought a pair of toy store walkie-talkies so she could talk to me, in my bedroom, whenever she wanted.

"Calling Mom. Calling Mom," she'd say, sending shivers of love and excitement through my body.

"Come in, Missy! Come in!" I'd answer.

Then we'd talk over the radio, through the thin wall between us, for hours. Until the batteries got faint or we fell asleep. Within a few weeks, I was like her big sister. Within a few years, I thought, I could actually become her real mother again.

She made friends with the neighborhood children. Connie loved her like her own daughter. Missy asked me once whether Connie and I loved each other.

"Yes, sweetie," I said.

"Like a boy and a girl?"

"Well, sweetie, yes. Something like that."

"Well, then, is Connie a boy?"

"No, she's not."

"She looks like a boy, though."

"Well, she isn't. But that doesn't matter. She loves me just the same."

We blushed and giggled. That was about as far as we got. I suppose as the years went by I would have had to explain things further. But I didn't get the chance.

After about six months my mother started calling me, describing disgusting things she said she knew were going on between Connie and me. Somehow she'd got it into her mind that we were mistreating Melissa, exposing her to sex and drugs and whatever else entered her imagination. She threatened to call the police and have them arrest us.

I got so angry and scared that I hung up on her. I trembled. This *was* Texas, Connie and I *were* lesbians, and she probably could get us arrested—in front of Melissa—if she wanted to.

It was like walking a tightrope with Melissa in my arms. I tried to control myself and tell her that everything was all right. That all the things she accused me of were just figments of her imagination.

But she kept calling, again and again, and Melissa heard more and more of our arguments. She asked about her grandma, often. I lied and told her everything was fine.

Then my worst fear came true. Mary Mildred showed up one night, with Raymond waiting outside in the car, and threatened to call the cops if we didn't send Melissa home with her. Right this minute. Now.

Melissa saw it all. I don't know how much she really understood. She hugged her grandmother.

"What should I do, Mommy?" she asked me.

I searched my heart. It hurt. I tried to think of the best thing I could do for my daughter. There were no good choices, none at all. Shouldn't I, her real mother, hold on like a mother bear or a she-lion? Could I even think of abandoning her to this terrible woman? Could I risk having her, along with Connie, dragged through the courts and see all of our private lives spilled out into the open? If I wanted to fight for her, to keep her with me, wouldn't I have to teach her to hate and fear my mother, as I did?

In the five minutes I had to decide I chose the path that I thought would hurt Missy the least. I think it was the right one. The worst part is, I'll never really know.

"Go along with Grandma," I said. "We'll be together again soon."

She kissed me and left her mother's house. For as long as I could stand it, I kept her room ready for the day she would come back. Gradually, the pain in my soul shrank down into its own private space.

The years rolled on. My mother moved from house to house, from city to city, just as often as before. Missy became a voice on the phone.

Connie and I gradually turned our cleaning business into a small construction company. We taught ourselves how to texture and dry-wall and worked side by side rehabilitating apartment buildings.

We didn't even have to talk to each other. We could communicate our needs without speaking. I learned how to estimate the cost of jobs and materials. Lots of the building owners I talked to were surprised to see a woman instead of a man show up. I set them straight.

The business grew. More and more people hired us. Soon we

were employing people ourselves—carpenters, electricians, labor-
ers. Usually, they were drifters and outcasts and people who had
known trouble, like ourselves.

There was Joe Brown, a young-old middle-aged man who'd had
a heart attack and who kept house for us. There was Lee, a carpen-
ter, who looked just like Jesus Christ. He drifted in and out of our
lives for years.

There was Kimberly, who was eighteen, the beautiful daughter
of a rich Houston man, a lawyer. Kim had run away from home and
gotten into and out of drugs and other terrible things, and then
she found us. In the evenings, after she'd put in her day working
for us as a laborer, we'd sit and talk about her troubles. She went
through a long time when she couldn't sleep. She'd knock on our
door in the middle of the night.

"Grandma, I can't sleep. Can I come in there with you and
Grandpa?"

"Yes, Kimberly," I'd say.

She would crawl in with Connie and me, and I would turn on
the TV to help chase away her demons. We would all wait together
for the dawn.

Having Joe and Lee and Kim and the others was almost like
having a real family. I tried to keep it together as best as I could.

As for my other life, as Jane Roe, it faded into the background
but never really went away. When I could I kept up, in the newspaper and on television, with all the new political fights over abortion.

I got mad that *Roe* v. *Wade* was being challenged. I agonized
over the trouble the pro-choice people were having—and worried
if my identity, or my lie about being raped, would be discovered,
whether it would hurt the pro-choice cause, somehow. I worried
about this a lot. But I didn't talk about it with anyone. I kept quiet.
I kept my head down. When the pressure inside got too great, I lost
my temper about other things, little things, and yelled at Connie or
the kids. Or I drank.

Sometimes I wondered if there was anything, as Jane Roe or
just plain Norma McCorvey, I should be doing for the pro-abortion
cause. Other times—remembering my run-in with the women's
rights leader who didn't believe I was Jane Roe—I just wished that

she was right, that I wasn't really Jane Roe. Or that I had been Jane Roe, but that I wasn't her anymore: the people who knew me by that name had long since forgotten about me or had picked someone else to take my place.

But that was just a fantasy. One day in 1984, with no warning, a letter came to the house. It was from Sarah Weddington, whom I hadn't talked to in years and years, and she was asking for my help.

~16~

By the early 1980s, the news that *Roe* was in serious, serious trouble had even reached my world. It was obvious to everybody everywhere that the right to choose abortion—which had seemed so absolutely final, so completely invincible, only ten years ago—was in danger of being wiped away.

The problem wasn't that most people in America weren't in favor of choice. They were. The problem was that the minority of people who were anti-choice were suddenly more organized and more committed to fighting.

After 1973—after the "final" abortion battle had been won—many pro-choicers gave up their political activism, or turned their attention to other women's issues like the Equal Rights Amendment, or concentrated on their families or careers. (Sarah Weddington, for instance, left the Texas legislature in the mid-1970s and went to Washington to work in Jimmy Carter's administration.)

That left a vacuum, which was filled by the minority of anti-abortion activists. Many of these people—devout Catholics, Fundamentalist Christians, anti-feminists, and out-of-power conservatives in search of a hot issue—had been shocked that their idea of what constituted sin, shame, and murder had been denied by the highest court in the United States. They felt "compassion" for women who needed abortions, but they felt a lot more strongly that it was their duty to bring the rest of the country around to their way of thinking. In other words, make abortion illegal all over again.

They began to organize, just as the pro-choice groups had done, and started to make their plans for overturning *Roe* v. *Wade*. *Roe*'s weak spot, as they saw it at first, was that the Court's decision left some room for individuals to regulate the legal practice of abortion.

So several conservative state legislatures passed laws nibbling away at women's rights. If these laws had gone into effect, in certain states women wanting abortions would have had to get their husband's permission—or their parents', if they were minors—or get their abortions done in expensive hospitals, wait for two or twenty-four or forty-eight hours after their first visit to an abortion clinic, or be "counseled" by anti-abortion activists before they underwent their procedure.

All the anti-choice laws were overturned by the Supreme Court. But in the U.S. Congress, where noise and money can oftentimes get things done, the story was different.

In 1976 Henry Hyde, a Republican congressman from Illinois, attached an amendment to a budget bill. It prohibited the federal government from allowing Medicaid funds to be used to pay for abortions. The Hyde Amendment meant that poor women, the kind who needed help in getting abortions the most, could not have their abortions paid for by a government health plan. The Hyde Amendment passed, and by a five-to-four decision it was declared constitutional. The people least able to defend themselves began to suffer the most.

Excited by their success, the anti-choice groups stepped up their political activity. They raised more and more money for gruesome anti-choice leaflets, movies, and TV commercials, filled with blood and dead fetuses blown up to hundreds of times their actual size. Abortion clinics were picketed. Clinic patients and doctors and staff members were harassed. Sometimes, even the entrances to the facilities were blocked.

Then, in 1980, a politician named Ronald Reagan, an ex-movie actor and a friend of many rich people and TV preachers, declared himself in favor of "the humanity of the unborn" and promised to choose only anti-*Roe* judges to fill vacancies on the Supreme Court if he was elected president.

He was. During his presidency, he addressed several anti-*Roe* rallies, and even prohibited the United States from paying for teaching birth control techniques in poor countries overseas. By the early 1980s, many of the judges who had voted for *Roe* were nearing retirement age and Ronald Reagan was poised to name their replacements.

In January 1984, a former car salesman turned Fundamentalist Christian speaker named Randall Terry heard God speaking to him in the back of a chartered bus driving home from an anti-choice rally in Washington. In this vision, God told Terry to form an organization dedicated to stopping women from getting abortions. No matter what the consequences.

He decided to call his group "Operation Rescue."

✑ 17 ✑

The letter from Sarah Weddington was from Massachusetts, written on the stationery of a famous college, where she'd just given a speech. Sarah wrote that a TV reporter from Channel 8 in Dallas had called her office and asked her to get in touch with Jane Roe. This reporter was doing a news report the new abortion fight and wanted to include me in it. If I wanted to be interviewed, said Sarah, I should call the reporter at her TV station. If, of course, I wanted to go public.

If I wanted to go public. The sentence leapt off the piece of paper and into my brain. After a frozen moment of fear and jumbled thoughts, the question was just as unanswerable as the ones I'd tried to bury behind me. After all these years of running—trying to look only straight ahead, not behind—the past and present were exploding together.

Did I want to go public? Did Norma McCorvey? Did Jane Roe?

No. Norma McCorvey was a scared and angry cleaning woman, a person who was just trying to get through the day without crying or shouting or drinking herself unconscious. There was no way Norma McCorvey could talk to smart people or rich people. No way she could expose herself to their stares and questions and accusations. No way she could let them force out her horrible secrets.

But then, from somewhere deep inside me, somewhere surprising, the other woman—the one whose name was on the Supreme Court papers, and someday, maybe, in the history books— raised her voice.

"Yes," whispered Jane Roe.

Her voice was calm, reasonable. Like I'd always wanted mine to be. Although nobody knew her, she said, Jane Roe really existed. In her own way, Jane Roe was a survivor, a fighter. Maybe it's time she stopped hiding. Maybe it's time she got involved in the cause. Maybe it's time we stood in the spotlight. Maybe it's time we stood up. Maybe it's time we let ourselves be known. To be a little proud of ourselves.

Maybe it's time.

When I finally called the station, after three or four weeks of worrying and sleepless nights, Uma Pemmarju, the reporter from Channel 8, was glad to hear from me. She asked me out to lunch. She told me how worried she was about all the bombings and pick-etings at the abortion clinics, how brave I'd been to do what I'd done.

Uma was a beautiful woman, with exotic olive-colored skin. She told me that the reason she had a strange name was that both her parents were from India. Even so, she talked like a Texan. She told me that I could trust her because she was pro-choice—but that as a reporter, she wouldn't let that affect her.

I didn't totally understand what she meant by that. But finally, after a few more conversations, I said that it was okay if she asked me questions about the things she had talked about: my reaction to all the terrible things the anti-choice people were doing.

The interview day arrived. I put on my best T-shirt and jeans. The truck from the TV station drove up and parked right in front of our house. The neighbors stood outside to watch the show through our front windows.

To get thirty seconds of air time, it took four hours. Every time Uma's camerawoman started shooting me, I got sick to my stomach and ran to the bathroom to throw up.

"What are you frightened of?" asked Uma.

I was scared of telling a lie. Or maybe, of telling the truth.

"I don't know," I told her.

"What can I do to help?" she asked.

She couldn't. On that endless afternoon I could think of only one answer to my panic. During one of my trips to the bathroom I took some old, bootleg Valium pills. I went to the kitchen and drank a glass—two glasses—full of vodka.

After a little while, though still scared, I could just about manage to sit still for Uma's questions. I answered them as best I could, with the answers I thought would be best for the pro-choice cause. I told her how angry and depressed I'd been because I hadn't been able to get an abortion. How glad I was that the Supreme Court had voted for "my law" and how angry and depressed I was, again, that the anti-choice people were closer and closer to getting it overturned.

Uma was happy. She and her assistants packed up their equipment and left.

That night, Connie and I stretched out on our couch and watched me say my thirty seconds' worth on television. Then we braced ourselves for the next day. For the backlash. For people to point me out on the street, throw garbage on our lawn, paint hateful words on our garage door, or burn down the house.

Nothing like that happened, though. Not for a while, anyway.

What happened next was that both Jane and Norma—but mostly Jane—inched out of the closet and into whatever part of the public imagination that was reserved for people like us. Other reporters came over to the house, or phoned, and though I was always just as sick and scared as the first time, the interviews went pretty well.

Most of the reporters told me, as Uma had, that they were secretly pro-choice. What they really wanted from me, I figured out, were a few good pro-choice slogans, attached to a description of me as a normal poor Texas woman who, for normal reasons, had lived a very hard life. When their questions touched on the parts of me that didn't fit it wasn't hard to steer them away.

Sometimes it seemed that the interviewers were the ones doing the steering. That they were just as eager to stay clear of my dark side as I was. Which made me a little less nervous.

But afterwards, thinking about what I'd said and left unsaid, I worried. What good was I doing? What example was I setting? In the long run, what good would come from passing off half-truths and coverups? What would happen to me, or the pro-choice movement, if someone actually dug up the truth and threw it in my face?

And underneath it all, what would it do to me, what would I turn into, if I had to spend my life hiding most of myself, in plain sight?

What eventually happened was something different—something I hadn't anticipated and couldn't control.

My world got bigger, quickly. It had to, to include more and more people. The people who knew me because I was Jane Roe. Some of them liked me and some of them hated me. And others had thoughts about me I couldn't figure out at all.

The first pieces of hate mail began to find their way to our mailbox. The letters were usually scrawled, mostly misspelled, on school notebook paper with Magic Marker or pencil. They weren't signed. They called me a baby killer, evil, and much, much worse. These letters chilled my blood.

About a year after my interview with Uma, somebody—Connie and I never found out who—began scattering articles of dolls' clothing, tiny dresses, on our front lawn. We woke up, looked out the front window, and saw them lying there. The same person, or someone different, later overturned our garbage cans and scattered the contents in front of our door for Connie and me to clean up when we came home from work.

I guess this was some kind of symbolic statement about abortion. There was no note, no explanation. Whatever the message was, it scared us. But there was no turning back.

When I think back on it now, it was three people who were mainly responsible for helping me see that I had a place in the big world. Their names are: Fred Friendly, Michael Manheim, and Carl Rowan.

Fred Friendly was a famous television news producer who lived in New York. He'd produced most of the news specials for CBS in the 1950s, and he had even been the president of all of CBS News in the 1960s. By the time I met him he had retired from television and was a journalism teacher at Columbia University.

Out of the blue, Fred phoned me in Dallas. He was, he said, writing a book called *The Constitution: That Delicate Balance.* It was about important court cases that had gone to the Supreme Court and the people behind them. He wanted me to come to New York so he could interview me for it. He would send me my ticket. And oh, yes—when I got off the airplane at Kennedy Airport, I should look for a person holding a sign that said "McCorvey."

"Okay?"

The way Fred said it, he made it sound as if what he was asking me to do was to travel from one end of my living room to another.

It was my second trip in an airplane. The only other time I had flown was when I was running away from Woody McCorvey. This time I wasn't numb. I was shaking with nerves. By the time the plane was over New York City, I had convinced myself I'd been a sucker, there would be no one to meet me, and I would be lost, mugged, and robbed in the first five minutes.

"Hello! You must be Norma," said the nice middle-aged woman holding the sign that said "McCorvey" at the gate.

Her name was Ruth Friendly. She was Fred's wife. She helped me get my bags and took me outside to a car—not just a taxi but a hired car—that was waiting for us. We drove up to their big house in Scarsdale, in the suburbs.

I stayed with them, in their guest bedroom, for nearly a week. Fred had his office, filled with books and plaques and other awards he'd won, right there in the house. We talked for a few hours every day.

Fred seemed old to me. He was a tall, gray-haired man who wore a suit even in his own house. But he listened as politely, as interestedly, as *hard* to me as anyone had ever done. Then he told me stories about himself: mostly about old television news shows he'd done with his best friend, Edward R. Murrow. It was plain to me that Edward R. Murrow, who even I remembered watching on television, was his hero as well as his friend. Edward R. Murrow had died a few years before, although I didn't remember it happening, and Fred missed him.

When we were finished, Fred took me to his journalism classroom at Columbia so he could introduce me to his graduate students. They looked so smart and young and sure of themselves that I was excited and intimidated and angry, all at once. Some of them asked me for my autograph. Were they making fun of me? A part of me thought so. But another part thought, maybe not.

Even in the middle of New York City, Fred had treated me like a grownup, introducing me to his friends and students as an important person with something valuable to say. Ruth Friendly was also kind to me. She took me around Manhattan. She walked fast, her eyes straight ahead, knowing exactly where she was going—right through all the waves of incredible sights and smells and sounds that I couldn't even begin to take in, much less sort out.

One evening, Ruth took me to dinner at Windows on the World, a fancy restaurant on top of the World Trade Center, the tallest building in New York. The next day she took me shopping—to some of the big, famous department stores, most of which we just walked around in. I told Ruth that I wanted to buy something for Melissa, who was going to be sixteen soon. She steered us to Tiffany's, on Fifth Avenue, which I'd heard about even back in Dallas. It was just as beautiful as I'd imagined it. The man at the door was huge. He wore a tall red hat, like a London palace guard.

I thought: I bet that's the same man who opened the door for Audrey Hepburn in *Breakfast at Tiffany's*. I bought Missy a little silver half-ounce perfume decanter that she could carry in her purse. It was so tiny and lovely and feminine that it made me cry.

Michael Manheim was a Hollywood movie producer. Before I'd met him, he'd worked on television movies and specials for other people. Now he had his own company.

Michael Manheim called me up one day and told me he'd like to talk to me about making a movie about *Roe* v. *Wade*. He wanted to know if he could meet me and talk over the idea.

I liked the sound of his voice, and told him so. He flew to Dallas and surprised the hell out of Connie and me. When both of us imagined meeting a movie producer, we thought we'd be meeting a bald-headed man with a big potbelly who smoked cigars and wore dark glasses. But Michael was young and thin and wore blue-jeans and a T-shirt. He sat on our living room couch and talked about the years he'd lived with the Navajo Indians.

He said he believed in a woman's right to abortion—in fact, he'd done his college thesis on women's reproductive rights. He said that abortion was one of the most important, controversial, and interesting issues of the age.

He talked some more about feminism. We asked him all about making movies in Hollywood. We asked him if he'd met Jane Fonda and Mickey Rooney. He said he had.

I'd had some bad late night fears that a dishonest moviemaker would steal my story. But after meeting Michael, I wasn't as worried. For months after he flew back to Los Angeles, he would call me up to talk some more about the movie. He asked me: What did I think about making the story about me and Sarah and Linda, all together? I told him that sounded fine.

Michael said that making a movie like this would take a great deal of money and time. I said I understood. Although, of course, I really had no idea at all.

By the mid-1980s, the cost of buying workman's compensation insurance had forced us to shut down our renovation business. Connie worked for a construction company, putting up drywall. I managed several apartment buildings in one of the poor neighborhoods where we used to do housecleaning.

Then one day Michael Manheim called. "Norma, I really feel that Debra Winger should be the actress playing you," he said to me over the phone one night.

It was about then that I began to think of this movie as something that was actually going to happen. I told Michael I thought I should find someone to help me sell my story. He said he thought that was a good idea.

I asked Joe Floyd, the only lawyer I knew besides Sarah and Linda, where we could find an attorney who handled show business contracts. It wasn't all that easy to find one in Dallas. Finally, we located a man who said he could help us.

He negotiated a deal that said that after the movie was made I would get 60 percent of all the money paid out to the people portrayed. Sarah and Linda would each get 20 percent.

Before the movie was made, all three of us got "option" money. Mine came to about $3,000. We were also paid consultant fees for telling Michael and his scriptwriter our stories. My consultant fee was $35 an hour. Sarah and Linda each got $125 an hour, because that was their usual rate as lawyers.

All in all, over the years I've earned a little more than $50,000 for my part in what would become *Roe* v. *Wade*, the movie that aired on NBC television in 1989.

One day in 1986 we all met in Linda's law office to sign the contracts. I hadn't seen Sarah and Linda for seven years. During the meeting, Sarah pulled me aside and asked me what I was doing with my movie consultant fee. I said I hadn't decided yet. She strongly suggested to me that I should do what she was doing, which was to donate the money to the National Organization for Women. I'm sorry to say that this suggestion made me lose my temper.

Thanks to the movie money, Connie and I were able to buy health and car insurance for the first time. We went to the dentist and had our teeth fixed. Other incredible things began to happen.

Whatever parts of my life went into the movie went through Michael Manheim. During the months after the contract was signed, we spent hours and hours on the telephone, talking about my life between 1969 and 1973. Those were the lawsuit years, the ones the movie would be covering. Michael explained to me that he would pass on what I told him to the scriptwriter, a woman named Alison Cross. Alison took the parts of my life she could use and wove them into the story.

After awhile, actual movie scripts came for us to read. Version after version. Change after change. Via Federal Express, marked *Urgent*. Connie and I would sit in the living room, reading and making notes. Then I'd call Michael in Los Angeles and read the notes to him. Mainly my suggestions had to do with what I was wearing, or where I would go, or how I had said a certain thing back then. Sometimes my suggestions would go into the next version. Sometimes they wouldn't. Other times, whole new characters or plot twists would pop up, or old ones would disappear completely. Michael explained that a lot of the changes were because the network knew this was going to be a controversial movie and wanted to handle things just right.

In fact, Michael said, a lot of anti-choice groups were trying to get NBC to cancel *Roe* v. *Wade* even before it was made. They "knew" the movie would be pro-choice—liberal propaganda in favor of killing unborn babies. There was a lot of pressure on both

him and the network to be "fair." The anti-choice groups would
love to get their hands on our project and tear it apart.

That's why, he said, he was keeping what was in the movie a
secret until the absolute last possible moment. It was the reason
why none of the scripts he sent us were titled *Roe* v. *Wade*. That way,
nobody looking to steal one would find it. Michael made up all
sorts of fake names for the scripts: *Untitled*; *The Norma McCorvey
Story*; and one that especially sticks in my mind, *An American Story*.

Carl Rowan was a famous reporter, an expert on politics who
wrote a column for a Washington newspaper that was reprinted all
around the country. In 1987, he was working on a public television
program called "Searching for Justice." The show would be introduced by Thurgood Marshall, one of the Supreme Court justices
who voted to legalize abortion.

"Searching for Justice" was the story of three ordinary
Americans who took their cases to the Supreme court. It reminded
me of Fred Friendly's book. But Carl Rowan didn't remind me of
Fred.

Carl Rowan was a middle-aged black man who wore white suits
and big white Panama hats. At least he did when he was on television. He was very smart, and very cool. When he came down to
Dallas to shoot me he stayed at a fancy hotel, and when he took me
out to dinner we ate and drank up more expense account money
than I'd thought was possible.

Why I chose to unburden myself to Carl, after fourteen years, is
still a mystery to me. But I'm glad that he was there to give me the
chance. Maybe it was just my time to come out. I was tired of hiding so many things from so many people. I was tired of drinking
and taking pills to calm myself for interviews. I was tired of bracing
myself for the question that I knew had to come.

If Carl had told me it was coming in advance, I might have
reacted differently. But Carl didn't warn me. The cameras were set
up in the house, as always, and as always I'd had to swallow some
Valium and vodka. About thirty minutes into the interview, Carl
looked at me and said: "Norma, let's talk about the rape."

I didn't think. I just answered with the truth. "Carl, I wasn't
raped," I said. Then I explained that I'd lied, all those years ago
with Sarah and Linda, and why I had done it.

Carl got up from his chair. "Cut," he said. His assistant asked if she could use my phone to call someone.

Carl asked me if that was the truth, what I really wanted to say. I told him it was. And the miracle was, I was sitting there very calmly. I'd stopped shaking. I no longer felt nauseated. My headache suddenly disappeared.

I'd done it. Why did I feel so good?

Connie called me into the bedroom to talk to me privately. "Do you realize what you just said?" And I said, "Yes."

It was as simple as that. The next day, there was an article on the front page of the *Morning News*. The headline was: "Roe v. Wade Plaintiff Says She Lied About Rape."

I braced myself for the worst. But amazingly, there was very little about the possibility of the decision being overturned. A man they interviewed in the newspaper, from the district attorney's office, said that since the old Texas anti-abortion law made no exceptions for rape, it didn't matter how I got pregnant. Sarah issued a statement calling my rape lie "irrelevant."

In the next few days I got lots of calls from reporters about the issue. They all seemed to understand why I lied. Some even understood how and why I'd agonized about it. There were a few more articles published. And then, silence.

The cloud of gray that had been such a big part of my life tore itself into little pieces and went away. In my sudden happiness, I could see something very clearly: I wasn't quite as much a freak, a misfit, as I thought I was.

What I'd done was wrong, but it almost certainly wasn't a mistake out of the bounds of human behavior. I hadn't cut myself loose from the human race—or rather, if anyone had done anything like that, it was myself.

The fact was, I was one of the women affected by *Roe* v. *Wade*. And I knew almost nothing more about it except what I had seen with my own two eyes. For the first time, I was curious. I went to the library and checked out some books on women's rights.

"Have you ever heard of Holly Hunter?" Michael Manheim asked me. I told him I was sorry, I hadn't.

Michael explained that she was a very, very good actress whom he wanted to play me in the movie. He told me that she had a very funny movie called *Raising Arizona* in the theaters at the moment, and a very good movie called *Broadcast News* on videotape. Connie and I saw both movies—and after we did, we both fell in love with Holly Hunter. We thought she was the cutest little thing since buttons.

In *Raising Arizona*, I loved how she didn't take any static from her husband's stupid gangster-type friends. In *Broadcast News*, I liked how she was able to deal with the tension of her job by taking her phone off the hook, crying for exactly one minute, and then start right in as a newswoman again.

I didn't think I looked particularly like her in either of those movies. But I certainly wouldn't have minded if I had.

Michael's plan was that Holly Hunter would come down to meet me before she started playing me in the movie. Holly's brother, it turned out, lived just a few miles from us. So she could stay at his house, borrow his car for the day, and drive herself over.

On a Saturday morning just like any other one—except for the fact that we were out of our minds with excitement and nervousness—Connie and I added a rug shampoo to the normal house cleaning routine, and waited. Right on the dot, she pulled into our driveway. For the rest of day, we sat and talked and exchanged memories.

At first, Connie and I couldn't get over how a movie star had driven up to our front door and, sitting on our old couch, turned into a real person right in front of our eyes. But after a while a strange and wonderful thing happened: Holly Hunter and I just seemed to melt together.

I told Holly some things about my childhood in Texas and Louisiana and a lot of what was going on with me during the years the movie covered. Holly told me about growing up in Georgia. She'd had a rough time herself, she said. Her stories weren't quite as bad as mine, but I gave my word that I wouldn't repeat them. I haven't. I will say, though, that Holly's politics were strictly pro-choice. That was one of the main reasons, she said, that she'd decided to do the movie.

Since the carnival I'd worked for was in the last version of the movie I'd read, I stood up right there in the living room and did my whole freak show spiel from memory for her. Holly laughed and applauded—and then stood up and did it herself.

As the day went on and we kept talking, Holly began sounding more and more like me. Out of the corner of my eye, I could see her checking out my gestures and movements and beginning to do them herself. It was the strangest thing—like looking into a mirror and seeing another person.

By the end of the day we were just like girlfriends. As the evening wore on, our stories—about my attempts to give interviews and be famous, about her attempts to deal with the crazy movie people who somehow always got to work on all her pictures—got funnier and funnier. I brought out some old snapshots to show her. And oh, by the way, I said, did she know I still had a lot of the clothes and stuff from my hippie days?

Holly got excited when she heard that. Could she possibly see those things? she asked.

I took her by the hand, pulled her back into my bedroom, and rooted around deep in my closet until I got to some of my old halter tops and headbands and hippie jewelry.

I told her: "I'm going to give these to you, and if Michael doesn't object I want you to wear them in the movie."

Holly promised that she would.

"It'll make it way more interesting, Norma," she said. And movie star or not, she kept her promise.

It was a strange and exciting feeling knowing that somebody, somewhere, standing in front of a movie camera, was acting and talking just like me. Even stranger was the idea that the anti-choice people seemed to be angrier at the make-believe Norma than they'd ever been at me.

It made them go berserk that the story of our winning the lawsuit would actually get told on national television. Michael and his movie people were getting all sorts of grief. I could hear the tension in his voice over the telephone. The anti-choicers were still putting pressure on the network to pull his plug. Sometimes, he told me, protesters managed to get ahold of his secret location addresses and shut down filming for the day.

But like the case itself, *Roe* v. *Wade* kept moving forward despite all the obstacles in its path. Michael flew Connie and I out to Los Angeles for a few days, to meet the cast and take publicity pictures.

Connie talked to the woman who was playing her—Kathy Bates, who became much more famous a couple of years later.

The filming finished. Sweet Holly—and all the other actors, I guess—went on to other jobs. Instead of scripts, Michael began to send me tape cassettes of versions of the movie he'd put together.

As it turned out, most of what went on the screen actually happened to me—but, for complicated reasons that had to do with television movie storytelling, a lot was rearranged and a lot more was left out. It wasn't entirely my story. The woman in the movie wasn't a lesbian, at least as far as the audience could see, and Jane Roe's struggles with drugs and alcohol and personal demons—and for the most part, with Sarah and Linda—weren't shown.

Because of that, and also to preserve what was left of my privacy, the Jane Roe in the movie was called "Ellen Campbell." I had mixed feelings about that. But when it was all over, I decided that I wouldn't have minded meeting Ellen Campbell one day. I owe her a lot.

Something puzzled me, though: *Roe* v. *Wade* was supposed to be a two-hour TV movie, but the tapes Michael sent me were never that long.

"Don't worry, Norma," he laughed. "We might just put in some commercials, too."

Actually, a lot of the movie's sponsors were nervous about possible boycotts threatened by the protesters. But the president of NBC, Robert Wright, stood up against censorship. He issued a press statement saying that *Roe* v. *Wade* would be shown in its entirety on the Monday evening for which it was scheduled, and that if sponsors wanted to pull out, that was fine. Some did; some didn't. I sent Mr. Wright a telegram: "Thank you very much for sticking to your guns. You're a true man. Hope we can meet in the near future. Jane Roe."

I never did meet Mr. Wright. When the final version arrived, it was just Connie and me in the living room. I'd taken $900 of my consultant money, bought a brand-new 25-inch television, and had it delivered to the house. We turned off the telephone for the two hours the movie was on. I cried for most of that time.

Roe v. *Wade* was a wonderful movie. But the world doesn't need me to tell it that. The world can see that for itself, and it has. *Roe* v. *Wade* won two Emmy awards in 1990. I'm happy for everyone who worked on it that it turned out so well.

From my point of view, what I can truly tell everyone about the movie is that what Michael said would happen, happened. Parts of my life—some of them, like the birth scene of the *Roe* baby, so accurate that I could feel the horror all over again— were used to tell a very important story.

I recognized that woman up on the screen. She was me, taken apart and pasted back together again with most of the rough edges cut off. Which naturally got me to wondering: Was "Ellen Campbell" the roughest version of Norma McCorvey that the world could stand to watch? Or did it mean that once they got used to the movie version, they wouldn't be as shocked if they eventually learned the real truth?

I couldn't decide. But the problem stayed with me. It stayed with me even as the commotion about the movie made me a little more famous myself.

Through local women's groups, I began to get invitations to meetings and rallies, to meet people and to speak in front of them, as best as I could. I went to colleges, women's clubs, even elementary schools—and, once, a Catholic elementary school! During these events I said as little as possible about my life and as much as possible about the pro-choice cause. The nervousness and nausea were bad, but afterwards I was always glad I'd fought my way through it.

In my spare time, I studied more and more about the women's and pro-choice movements. I got out my copy of the *Roe* decision and read through it again with a dictionary alongside.

In April 1989 I was invited to attend a big and very important pro-choice march and rally in Washington, D.C. Connie and I had tickets to leave on April 6. In the early morning of April 4 we were still in Dallas, asleep.

The first shot woke me up. It went into the back window of our old car, shattering the glass to pieces. I heard the shotgun blast go off in my sleep, like a crack of thunder in a bright blue sky.

I got out of bed and went into the living room to investigate. The second shot went into our front door. I turned toward the sound, not quite understanding, and just stood there.

Connie came up behind me, threw her arms around me, and pulled me down to the floor.

"Duck! Duck! Duck!" she shouted. I heard a squeal of tires.

I thought it must be a pickup truck drag racing outside. And then there was another sound, another boom, much louder! The living room window exploded inward, in slow motion, like a horror movie. The pieces flew toward us.

I couldn't breathe, but I wasn't yet scared. Connie was covering me with her body. Once again, for me, time had stopped.

⮌ 18 ⮍

By the late 1980s, Randall Terry had perfected the techniques Operation Rescue would use to prevent women from getting abortions. His group is funded by donations—mostly obtained through Fundamentalist Christian and Catholic churches. Terry's strategies stretch and break the limits of civil disobedience. OR demonstrators swarm around abortion clinics, blocking entrances and lying down in front of cars, preventing women from getting treatment.

The group is run by a small circle of men. When Randall Terry picks a city to invade and clinics to harass, local pro-lifers—male and female—are recruited to help him. OR demonstrators are often arrested, and when they are, often refuse to give their names to the police.

In the past few years OR has staged "rescues" in dozens of cities across the country, including Atlanta, New York, Indianapolis, Wichita, Milwaukee, Boston, and Los Angeles. Usually, the arrival of OR picketers brings out an equal or greater number of pro-choice supporters who fight to keep the clinics open. Whether he'll admit it or not, Randall Terry has mobilized whole communities in favor of abortion rights. Whether Operation Rescue does the pro-life cause more good than harm is an interesting question.

* * *

Unfortunately, it is not one that pro-choicers have had the time or energy to debate. That's because abortion rights have been under political and legal attack, too.

In 1988, George Bush ran for president. In order to get the Republican nomination, the former supporter of *Roe* had to satisfy his party's right wing that he was a born-again pro-lifer. Bush made a sharp right turn, and during his campaign declared himself against the "immorality" of abortion.

When he made it into the White House, President Bush addressed anti-abortion rallies. He appointed long-time pro-lifers as attorneys general, who threw the weight of the U.S. government behind local anti-abortion laws. He prohibited scientific research on aborted fetal tissue and the importing and prescribing of RU-486, a French drug that made early abortions safe and inexpensive.

Worst of all, he nominated two Supreme Court judges who were no friends of choice or women's rights: David Souter, whose opinion on *Roe* was unknown, and Clarence Thomas, who I believe lied at his Senate nomination hearing about his determination to make abortion illegal again. Thankfully, these two judges were not yet on the court when the pro-lifers made their strongest legal challenge against abortion yet.

In 1986, conservative politicians in Missouri pushed a bill through the state legislature that prohibited every hospital that received public funds—in other words, nearly every hospital—from performing abortions. The new law also stopped any state employee from counseling a woman about abortion and required that all five-month and older fetuses be tested for "viability": the ability to live by itself outside the womb. The reason given for this was that pediatric medicine had advanced enough since *Roe* so that younger infants could be kept alive after premature birth.

The Missouri law also declared that, in the state of Missouri at least, human life began at conception. It was as close to a total ban on abortion as they could get.

The law was immediately challenged by local pro-choice activists. It was declared unconstitutional by a state judge, and that decision was upheld on appeal. In January 1989, the U.S. Supreme Court agreed to hear *Webster* v. *Reproductive Health Services*. *Webster* was William Webster, the attorney general of Missouri. Reproductive Health Services was the name of an abortion clinic whose founders, like me, had agreed to be the plaintiffs in a legal challenge.

It was almost like rolling back the clock sixteen years. Only this time, after nearly a decade of anti-choice U.S. presidents, the Supreme Court had what seemed to almost everyone a majority of anti-*Roe* judges.

The year 1989 was probably the lowest, most desperate and depressing period of the entire pro-choice movement. George Bush and his anti-choice conservatives were firmly in power. They had succeeded in painting pro-choice women as dangerous, anti-family radicals. The women's movement itself was divided over many issues, between straight women and lesbians and between the older and younger generation.

Many abortion rights activists thought that *Roe* v. *Wade* was doomed. The huge April 1989 rally in Washington that I had been invited to was a last-ditch attempt to demonstrate just how many supporters abortion rights really had.

Whether the 600,000 marchers had any effect will probably never be known. On July 3, 1989, the U.S. Supreme Court announced its ruling. It had voted five to four that all of Missouri's obstacles to abortion were constitutional. It refused to rule on whether life began at conception.

It was a terrible defeat for any poor Missouri woman who needed an abortion. Also, to any American woman who was interested in safeguarding her right to control her own body.

In fact, the Supreme Court nearly did what Chief Justice William Rehnquist dearly wanted to do: overturn *Roe* v. *Wade* completely. But Sandra Day O'Connor, the only woman justice, objected to taking that step. Only Rehnquist's need for her vote on the majority side stopped him from declaring *Roe*—and the fundamental right to abortion—null and void.

As it was, the Court had declared that any individual state could make it almost impossible for local women to get an abortion. Several conservative states passed laws imposing waiting periods and requiring that minors get their parents' written consent. In July 1992 the Court ruled in another major decision, *Planned Parenthood of Southeastern Pennsylvania* v. *Casey*, that all these restrictions—just like Missouri's—were constitutional.

Pro-lifer terrorists, only slightly more fanatical than the Operation Rescue activists, were now bombing and setting fire to abortion clinics all over the country. In January 1993, all of George Bush and Ronald Reagan's Supreme Court judges voted that an existing civil rights law could not be used to stop anti-choice protesters from blocking the entrances to legal abortion clinics.

At that moment, just about everyone wondered how our country had gone so far down the wrong road.

⇒ 19 ⇐

They never found the person—or people—who shot into our home. But I think it's safe to assume that the woman they were trying to scare or hurt or kill wasn't Norma McCorvey, a poor uneducated Texas building manager.

The woman they were aiming at was Jane Roe. She was the person whose name stood for change and women's rights. The woman who threatened all their old attitudes and prejudices.

But here is the miraculous part about that awful night: Jane Roe stood up for both of us. Instead of killing Jane Roe, or driving her deeper into hiding inside me, they made her stronger. It was Jane Roe who got me through the minutes and hours and months after those horrible thirty seconds. It was Jane Roe who finally found me some answers, and some peace. I hadn't known that she—we—were capable of that. It was a turning point.

Which is not to say that the horror of the shooting didn't hit me. All of me. I can still feel the fear and panic right now.

After the last shot, and the awful squeal of tires, Connie and I lay huddled together, flat on the floor, trembling. We clung to each other, our hearts pounding, our ears ringing with the gunshots. Trying hard to breathe as quietly as possible, listening.

Outside, all we could hear were barking dogs and distant cars. There was nobody outside to stop, or even see, anybody driving by. Was the shooter going to come back and attack us again?

After ten minutes, which felt like ten hours, I got up from the floor and dialed 911. A while later, a squad car pulled up. Two Dallas policemen got out and came inside. They didn't seem very excited about what had happened to us.

"Well, let me ask you," said one of them. "Did either of you girls just break up with somebody?"

Still in shock, Connie and I looked at each other and laughed nervously, an awful sound.

"Well, do either of you two women owe anybody any money?" he said.

The other cop went over to the shattered window, looked through it, and walked across the room to inspect the pellet holes in our walls. He took Connie into the bedroom.

"Why is he doing that?" I asked the policeman.

"He wants to see if your stories match up."

"Look," I said, finally, fighting for control. "you don't know what's really been going on."

I told him that although my name was Norma McCorvey, I was also Jane Roe, the woman in the big abortion case—and that was probably why our house had been attacked. When it sunk in who I was, the cop looked unhappy—even frightened—to be caught in this situation. He wanted no part of it, I could see. He backed away from me and tried to explain things to his partner.

Then, Jane Roe and I had our best and maybe bravest idea of the morning. I went to the phone, dialed information, and asked as calmly as I could, keeping my voice as normal as possible, for the number of the nearest FBI office. Even at five in the morning, somebody answered.

"FBI. Can I help you?"

"Yes, you can. My name is Norma McCorvey. Jane Roe in the Supreme Court case *Roe v. Wade*," I said.

Then I said that somebody had tried to scare or kill me. I wasn't sure which. Within a half-hour the house was surrounded by plain cars and I was talking to FBI agents in suits and ties. They were swarming over the house, looking for evidence, and the Dallas policemen faded gratefully into the background.

One of the FBI men made a special point of giving me his business card.

"My wife works for Planned Parenthood," he said.

"Does that make you pro-choice?" I said.

"Yes," he said, in a normal voice loud enough for everyone standing around us to hear.

By sunrise the TV trucks and reporters arrived. In a little while the FBI agents escorted us away, Connie out the front door, me out the back. They drove us, in separate cars, to separate hotel rooms.

Then I was alone. By mid-morning, the horror of the situation began to sink in. I needed Connie.

"Why have you separated us?" I asked the agent escorting me.

"Well, if they're out to get you, Ms. McCorvey," he said, "it's better that you be by yourself."

"Oh, yeah. I see," was all I could think to say.

Later, alone in my hotel room, I managed to call Connie, alone in hers. Finally, over the phone lines, we cried.

Two days later, in that week of fear and changes and miracles, Connie and I were in Washington, at the big pro-choice rally. We were surrounded by hundreds of thousands of women of all shapes and sizes and ages and colors—all of them come to defend something that I had helped start, over a little table in a pizza parlor, so many millions of years ago.

The rally was huge, too big for any one person to take in all at once. The crowds and the noise and the confusion scared me. And yes, I was still afraid that somebody out there was after me. But something else was happening, too.

Maybe the shooting had sent a shock through me and opened me up, because suddenly I saw that, in the middle of all the marchers, I didn't stand out in any bad or dangerous way. Yes, there were some women who looked richer or smarter than I did. But there were also a lot of women who looked a lot like me. Nobody pointed a finger to say that I was too poor, or too ignorant, or too queer or too selfish or too bad-tempered to march with them.

I felt part of something big, something important. I could feel the strength and love of the women gathered together that day, and I was part of that, too.

I felt anonymous and special, ordinary and famous, all at the same time.

Connie and I made our way up to the big tent near the side of the stage and looked in. At first, a bossy official told us we had no business being there. But when I told somebody else who I was, she went off and brought me a sash that said "V.I.P" and invited me up on the speakers' platform.

Nobody asked me to speak, but I stood up there listening to the speeches and cheers and music, and staring at celebrities like Jane Fonda, Barbra Streisand, Betty Friedan, and Jesse Jackson.

I'm sure that most of the people who saw me up there had no idea who I was. But nobody asked me to leave, either. Whether I was more nervous than excited, or more excited than nervous, was a good question. We left Washington for Dallas on a high, hardly thinking or talking about anything else.

When I got back the first thing I did was visit Melissa. She'd turned out fine and become a wonderful young woman, despite everything. She'd gotten married the year before and had just had her first child. My first grandchild.

She was the most beautiful baby I had ever seen. I brought the V.I.P sash with me to give to her. I draped it carefully, for a moment, around her pretty head. Then I left it with her mother, to keep it safe for her, until she was old enough to wear it herself.

After that, it seemed, Jane Roe was a bigger, more open, more powerful part of me than ever before. Maybe her real power was what kept the gunman from ever coming around to our door again.

Actually, I didn't do much thinking or worrying about him. I thought instead about the last twenty years—about struggling and failing and surviving and hiding. Especially hiding.

Now I realized that coming out of hiding, whenever I'd been brave enough to do it, hadn't hurt me nearly as badly as I'd feared it would. In fact, it was just the opposite. Staying hidden had been what had hurt me the most.

The truth was, that my deepest secret—that I was a poor, half-crazy, half-ordinary woman who'd been picked by fate to become a symbol of something much bigger and finer than herself—wasn't anything to be ashamed of.

I realized, finally, that I wasn't the wrong person to become Jane Roe. I wasn't the right person to become Jane Roe. I was just the person who became Jane Roe, of *Roe* v. *Wade*, the famous court case that freed women. And my life story, warts and all, was a little piece of history, no matter what I or anybody else said.

After that, it wasn't too long—maybe just a year or two—before I decided I should write this book. Before I could do that, I realized, I had to open up my life, and let myself and everybody else look into it, as much as I possibly could.

I came out as a gay woman in the fall of 1989. I decided to do it during an interview with a California newspaper. In interviews I've given and public situations I've been in since then, I've had few fears or problems about answering questions about my sexuality or my lifestyle. Or even, when the situation seems both comfortable and necessary, volunteering the information myself.

Coming out was one of the best decisions I've ever made. It has been surprisingly easy and painless. My friends and relatives had known about me for a long time. Their reactions I already knew, and I was already dealing with them the best I could.

The other people I told, the reporters and women's rights activists and even some pro-lifers, seemed less surprised that the person they were talking to was a lesbian than that I—and of course Jane Roe, too—had admitted it. Some, I could tell, thought that my being a lesbian made my story a lot more complicated to tell. I agree with them.

Other people have said me that being an open lesbian somehow hurts the pro-choice or women's rights causes. This confuses me, since lesbian liberation is a big part of the women's movement, and many women in the pro-choice movement are also lesbians. I can't see where telling people who I really am has so far hurt anything or anybody, in any way whatsoever.

In other areas of becoming Jane Roe openly, though, I decided that big changes were needed. I had to clean up my act in several important areas.

For most of my life, as anyone who's read this far already knows, I've hurt myself and the people around me with my drinking and drug use. For the last few years, with the help of some good friends, I've eliminated the first one and cut down drastically on the second.

Another problem, my temper, has been harder to control. But I try hard, and succeed a lot of the time in not giving in to it.

The next change might have been my biggest challenge. The decision to become a public person, to be a public speaker, is not easy for the part of me who thinks she's ignorant and knows she's mostly uneducated. I'm still very afraid of making mistakes and embarrassing myself, but I know, thanks to some very patient and supportive people, that it's possible even for someone like me to learn to handle the pressure well enough to say what needs to be said.

The first important person to help me in this area was Gloria Allred, a glamorous, smart, and fast-thinking attorney who's represented all sorts of oppressed and victimized people.

I met Gloria backstage at the 1989 pro-choice rally in Washington. Even though Gloria is an important and powerful person, she was excited to meet me and didn't talk down to me. We got along from the start.

After I got back to Dallas, we kept up talking to each other, on the phone, for hours. She's always been available to give me advice and help me plan my pro-choice strategy. It was her idea that I leave Texas and move to California, where she lives in Los Angeles, to get in touch with people who wanted to meet me and help me.

Gloria paid for my plane ticket to San Francisco. I settled in northern California, near a community consisting mostly of feminists and lesbians and strongly pro-choice women. I became great friends with Barbara Ellis, a wonderful older feminist who, along with her husband, John, a college teacher, took care of me and put me in touch with a lot of women's groups in the area.

It was at a meeting of pro-choice political workers that I met Mary and Frederick Gilmour, who run a public speaking school for businessmen and TV newspeople and other nervous people who need to get their point across. Since the Gilmours were strongly pro-choice—and generous people—they took me on as a scholarship student.

I'm sure I was their most backward student and biggest challenge. But I'm proud of what we did together. For three days I lived in Mary and Fred's house and worked with them, working on my concentration and pronunciation and meaning and looking at

awful videotapes of myself over and over and over. Until—a miracle!—I got some idea of what I was supposed to be doing there.

I realized I'd never be a Gloria Steinem or a Holly Hunter or a
Hillary Clinton or a Connie Chung, but I became as comfortable as
I'll ever be in front of a crowd of people. Or in front of a camera. I
learned to put up an invisible wall between myself and the audience, and after that, learned how to reach right through that wall.
My voice began to go up and down in mostly all the right places,
and my standard pro-choice speech—which I wrote, together with
my friends, around that time—began to sound, when I spoke the
words out loud, almost as good it looked on paper.

After I finished at the Gilmours' school, I felt almost qualified
to stand up in front of audiences, say what I wanted to say, and tell
them what I wanted them to know. So far, I've been pretty much
able to push down my fear and do it—at places as small and
friendly as a local women's club and as big and intimidating as
"Good Morning America."

All of which means that these days, Jane Roe and I have
become partners, sharing and helping each other when we need
to. It's not the most natural partnership in the world. A good
friend of mine, a writer who has worked in Hollywood and New
York, says that I am the only person he has met who is completely
famous and completely an ordinary, maybe even obscure person,
all at the same time.

That sounds about right. The last few years have been exciting,
working for the pro-choice cause, but that doesn't mean that the
troubles and demons in my own life have disappeared. I'm still
poor. I'm still looking for security. I'm still looking for love, maybe
more love than any one person has a right to. I'm still looking to
heal the hurting places inside of me.

Deep inside, I'm still nobody but Norma McCorvey.

The bad old Norma still makes appearances now and then. Her
habits are hard to break, damn it. She's quick, much too quick, to
imagine that people are taking advantage or making fun of her.
Then she loses her temper, and loses everything, just like in the old
days.

Several very smart and very patient people, who in the past few years have worked with me on pro-choice matters, are no longer my friends. I want to apologize for my anger and thank them for their help.

I also feel bad that I no longer work with the very generous and selfless women and men at the Dallas abortion clinic where I was a telephone counselor. The stress of dealing with dozens of anxious pregnant women every week stirred up too many memories all at once.

I am back now to cleaning and maintaining buildings. It is hard and lonely work, but it is necessary, and something I am good at. And who knows, maybe I am the most famous cleaning woman in America.

I still live with Connie Gonzalez, my life partner, in our little house on the outskirts of Dallas. I take care of Connie as best I can. Connie takes care of me, which is a much harder job. During the year and a half I was in California, we were separated. The strain of living together for a lifetime had gotten to be too much. But now we are trying again. Even if we fail, we will still be there for each other.

As for the other important women in my life, my daughter Melissa and I talk often—between the disagreements and silences that tear us up inside. My mother and I have many more things to work out before we can become friends. I hope we can begin the healing process soon.

Not a day goes by during which I don't think of my other two children. I wonder where they are, what they are doing right now, at this very moment, and whether giving them away guaranteed them a better life.

I hope it did. I hope they aren't angry at me for my many weaknesses and shortcomings. I also hope somehow they realize that their very first mother loves them very much, and always will.

The long silence between Sarah Weddington and me continues. Maybe this will help to end it: over the years, between our bursts of anger and resentment and jealousy, I've come to see us as two sides of the same coin, each with something equal and opposite—control and danger, wisdom and impulse, fire and ice—to bring to the most important event of our lives. Jane Roe, I'm certain, wouldn't have had a chance of making history without Sarah

Weddington. I hope that one day Sarah can bring herself to feel the same way about Jane.

About me, Norma McCorvey, too. Because I've finally come to realize this: without Jane Roe, without a cause to fight for and a purpose for living, the original Norma would never have survived.

Even in my loneliness, I was not alone. In my anger and joy and struggles I was connected—to all the women everywhere who have tried, in their own ways, to take off the handcuffs of the past and change their lives for the better. They could have gone along with the injustices of the past, held on to the old lies, and suffered in silence. But they let go, risking all they had, and fought for a better future. That was their choice. And mine.

～ 20 ～

In November 1992 the first pro-choice president in sixteen years was elected. Bill Clinton proved what pro-choice campaigners knew in their hearts all along: since the majority of Americans believe in the right to abortion, a pro-choice presidential candidate didn't have to duck the issue to win.

During his campaign, Clinton managed easily to be both "pro-family" and pro-reproductive freedom. He and Hillary Rodham Clinton spoke out frequently in support of *Roe* v. *Wade.*

In the days after his inauguration President Clinton fulfilled many of his campaign promises. He ended the "gag rule" on abortion counseling at government-supported hospitals. He stopped the ban on fetal tissue research and on importing the abortion drug, RU-486.

When Byron White, an anti-choice Supreme Court justice retired, President Clinton nominated Ruth Bader Ginsburg, a lawyer and fighter for women's rights, to fill his seat. Ruth Bader Ginsburg, unlike some of her predecessors, didn't hesitate a second at her Senate confirmation hearing to proclaim her view on choice—she is totally for it!

That makes one more precious vote for abortion rights. Overturning *Roe* seems to be a little less possible—for now. But anyone who thinks that the battle is even halfway over is just fooling herself.

In anti-choice states, the restrictions pushed through during the Reagan-Bush years are still on the books. In the U.S. Congress, there are still plenty of anti-choice legislators—enough of them to stop the Clinton administration from repealing the Hyde Amendment, which keeps poor women from getting abortions paid for by Medicaid. A proposed new federal law, the Freedom of Choice Act, which would guarantee all women the legal right to abortion, faces a long uphill battle.

And, of course, all over the country the anti-choice fanatics are still at work, still trying to inflict their own religious views on others, still trying to hide their anti-woman feelings, still trying to keep us from controlling our own bodies and our own lives.

On March 10, 1992, one of the more cruelly disturbed and ruthless members of this group murdered Dr. David Gunn, a passionately dedicated man who died helping to save the lives of the women he treated. It is for him—and all the others who gave their lives in pain and sadness, and yes, anger, before him—that we have to continue to fight.

The Jane Roe Speech

by

Norma McCorvey

Hello. I'm here today to tell you what it has been like to walk the path I, as Jane Roe, have traveled the last twenty years.

My journey began in 1969, not as Jane Roe, but as Norma McCorvey, a twenty-one-year-old woman with virtually no means of monetary support, no permanent place to live, many acquaintances, but no true friends. And I was pregnant, the unplanned result of a casual affair.

I was unaware of my pregnancy when I joined a carnival in August of 1969. I had been staying with my mother in Louisiana, but as usual, that situation didn't work out for very long. So, a more desirable alternative was to become a barker at the carnival that was in town. Not only was I a barker, but I also sold tickets to a freak animal show. There was an elephant-skinned dog, a five-legged steer, and a two-headed snake in a jar. I could relate to all the animals. Not only were we freaks of nature, but I could also feel their pain.

At the end of September, when the carnival was closing its seasonal tour in Fort Lauderdale, Florida, I began to feel some strange symptoms: morning nausea, headaches, ravenous hunger—and I realized that I hadn't had my period for nearly two months. I knew instinctively that I was pregnant.

I was out of a job, so I decided to return to Dallas, Texas, the city that I had lived in most of my life. An acquaintance wired me the bus fare, but I had no extra money for necessities like food or cigarettes. The bus ride to Dallas was long and lonely, but it gave me a lot of time to think about my future. I was furious because I had allowed myself to become pregnant. I thought to myself, disgustingly, about the pickle I was in. I had no job, no money, no friends, no place to live. My life was totally in limbo. I was feeling like getting the final bill and checking out. Suicide was beginning to look better and better.

When I got to Dallas, I lived in the women's lounge at the Greyhound bus station for five days. I knew that my father was somewhere in Dallas, but I was having trouble locating him. I stayed with acquaintances over the next month, and it was during that time that I found my father, and he consented to let me live with him.

Getting back to my pregnancy. I knew that I didn't want to carry the pregnancy to full term, but I didn't even know what the word was for termination of a pregnancy. I called the doctor that delivered my first child, and asked his nurse what the word was for ending a pregnancy. She spelled out the word A-B-O-R-T for me and suggested I look it up in the dictionary. I did look the word up, and knew then and there that's what I wanted. I called the nurse back and told her that I wanted an appointment to see the doctor to get an abortion. I didn't even realize that abortion was illegal.

I had talked to several women in my apartment building, and they had told me that the way to get an abortion was to say that I had been raped. So I devised a lie about a gruesome rape and presented it to a lawyer I consulted. His response was: "Did you file a police report?"

I was referred to Henry McCluskey, a Dallas attorney who handled adoptions. My hope was that he might know a doctor who did abortions. He informed me that abortion was illegal in the state of Texas. I had no money to travel anywhere else. The reality of my situation hit me like a ton of bricks. I cried for the next three days.

I asked around the neighborhood about abortion, and was told I could eat peanuts and drink castor oil, or throw myself down a staircase. The second alternative didn't sound too desirable, so I tried the first. I got very sick after eating all those peanuts with castor oil. But I was still pregnant.

I heard about an illegal abortion clinic in Dallas, and I went there, determined to get an abortion. When I got there I was shocked at what I found: the place was abandoned, the front door was off its hinges, a window pane was broken, dirty instruments were scattered around the room, and there was dried blood on the floor. I couldn't believe that women had actually come to this filthy place to get help. They must have felt they had no other alternative. I was desperate, too, but there was no one there to help me in my desperation.

I didn't realize it at the time, but the clinic had been busted. The feelings that I experienced then are equally real to me today: when I remember that miserable scene I become weak, sick to my stomach, scared, and extremely angry.

Shortly after this experience, Henry McCluskey referred me to Sarah Weddington and Linda Coffee. He told me that they were two young attorneys that were looking for a plaintiff to challenge the Texas abortion law.

After speaking with Sarah and Linda at a pizza place in Dallas, I agreed to be the plaintiff they needed to challenge the Texas abortion law. I still maintained hope that I would be able to achieve my goal: to terminate my pregnancy.

My contact with the two attorneys was very limited over the next two months. Time was heavy on my hands—every day was like a month to me. My depression became severe as it began to dawn on me that I possibly was going to have a baby.

Finally, after two months of sporadic contact with Sarah and Linda, I found myself in Linda's office, signing the appropriate papers to launch a lawsuit against Henry Wade, the district attorney in Dallas at that time. Just prior to signing the papers that brought *Roe* v. *Wade* into being, Sarah and Linda questioned me as to whether or not I still wanted to go through with being their plaintiff. My reply was: "Yes, let's do it for other women." But in my heart of hearts I still maintained the hope that I would be able to have an abortion. I didn't realize it at the time, but had I been able to obtain a legal abortion at that stage of my pregnancy, it would have involved major surgery—a Caesarean section.

It was at this meeting that the name "Jane Roe" came into existence. You may wonder why this name was used in the case instead of Norma McCorvey. I desired to remain anonymous for several reasons. My first concern was that I had five-year-old-daughter that

I did not want to entangle in politics. I did not want my parents to know about my involvement in the case because their religious background was clearly against abortion. I had lied about being raped, and was scared about the consequences of that action. So for these reasons, I didn't want my identity to be publicly known.

On March 3, 1970, *Roe* v. *Wade* was formally filed in the Dallas court system. I was six months pregnant.

From the time *Roe* v. *Wade* was filed in 1970 until the U.S. Supreme Court decision came down in 1973, I heard from Sarah Weddington and Linda Coffee on a very sketchy basis. I did not choose to participate in any of the court hearings because I wanted to keep my identity anonymous. I did not keep up with the progress of the case, except for occasional conversations with Sarah. She attempted to inform me about what was happening with *Roe* v. *Wade*, but she may as well have been speaking Greek to me.

In June of 1970 I went into labor at about two in the morning. My water broke and I began hemorrhaging. I woke my father up and he took me to the emergency room, only to find the emergency door of the small hospital locked. After an enormous amount of red tape concerning my giving the baby up for adoption, I barely had enough time to be prepped before giving birth. I asked the hospital staff if it was a girl or a boy, and they looked at me like I was from another planet. They refused to let me see the baby. In short, they made me feel like dirt. The next few days are fuzzy in terms of memory, but the one thing I do remember is when a nurse mistakenly brought my baby to my room. Needless to say, I was confused. When the nurse realized her mistake, she shot back into my room and snatched the baby out of my arms.

I was glad to be able to see the baby, but the experience was very difficult for me. I hope that women who choose adoption in this day and age are treated with more sensitivity than I was back then.

Two and a half years later, on January 22, 1973, in a short article on the lower right part of the front page of the Dallas *Times-Herald,* I read that abortion had become legal. The U.S. Supreme Court, in a seven-to-two decision, had ruled in favor of me in *Roe* v. *Wade.* My initial reaction was that I had been cheated, because I did not have a choice regarding my reproductive freedom. But I was happy that now my sisters would have a choice available to them.

For the next fourteen years I remained anonymous, except for very occasional appearances as Jane Roe.

In 1987 I consented to do an interview with Carl Rowan, a syndicated columnist. I was willing to do the interview, but was overwhelmed with fear regarding being questioned about the rape story I'd invented. Sure enough, the dreaded question came. Carl looked me right in the eye, and said, "Norma, let's talk about the rape," I looked right back at him and said, simply, "I wasn't raped." Needless to say, I shocked a few people. Personally, after telling the truth I felt like a mountain had been lifted off my shoulders.

Over the next few years, as I became aware of threats to abortion clinics and the actual bombing of the clinics, I began to participate more actively in the pro-choice movement. I started doing volunteer work at a Dallas women's clinic.

But it was not until early 1989 that I finally accepted myself as Jane Roe and stepped out of the political closet. I learned very quickly that there was a price to pay for this action. On April 4, just a few days before a huge pro-choice march in Washington, D.C., someone shot up my house and car. I was terrified, but even more determined to attend the march in Washington. My commitment to pro-choice began to surge.

Getting ready for the Washington march was a long and difficult process psychologically. I was still quite shaken from the April 4th incident. Frankly, I was afraid for my life.

On April 9, 1989, after participating in the march, I found myself on a stage on Capitol Hill, watching 600,000 people pouring through the streets of Washington, supporting women's equality and free choice regarding reproductive freedom. As I looked out at the multitude of people, the intensity of my feelings was overwhelming.

Here's what I feel. Decisions concerning childbearing are necessarily intimate, personal, and private. The Supreme Court recognized in 1973 that individuals, weighing their individual consciences, make better decisions than the state. Unfortunately, there are people who want to return to a time when this right was suppressed. If anti–free-choice forces are allowed to impose moral agendas on our society, we will lose the right to freely accept the responsibility for ourselves and our children.

They say that abortion is a controversial issue, but friends, let me tell you: privacy should not be controversial. It is a constitutional right. A human right.

This movement didn't start with me. I was just the straw that broke the camel's back. I fought back, and with the help of thousands who came before me, and on behalf of those who never came back—we won.

I remember the feelings I had when I walked into that illegal abortion clinic more than twenty years ago. I realized that the fear I experienced then was nothing compared to the feelings of the women that actually went through with illegal abortions. These women faced their deaths when they lay down on those tables in those back streets. They literally did not know if they would be alive in the next few hours, days, or weeks.

Prior to *Roe* v. *Wade*, approximately one million women had illegal abortions each year. Approximately 5,000 of these women were killed. Another 100,000 were hospitalized from botched abortions.

Obviously, abortion will continue whether it is legal or not. My concern is for the safety of millions of women should our freedom of choice be taken away from us. I want it clearly understood that I do not promote abortion. I promote personal choice.

If we return to the antique methods of dealing with unwanted pregnancies that existed before *Roe* v. *Wade*, the women's movement will be taking an enormous step backward. We are on the verge of having our reproductive freedom taken away from us if we do not take a stand and let our voices be heard NOW.

The future is YOUR hands. OUR hands. YOUR support of organizations like the National Abortion Rights League, Planned Parenthood, NOW, and the ACLU is crucial to our success. But the most important tool we have is inside each and every one of us: it is courage, commitment, and hope for the future.

When women bearing the torch of equality ran into the arena at the National Women's Conference in Houston, Bella Abzug said: "Some of us run with a torch. Some of us run for equality. But NONE of us runs for cover."

People of all nations who are pro-choice and pro-family, stand up and be counted. Support pro-choice candidates who are running for office. Write your state legislators and congressmen and congresswomen. Let them know exactly how you feel. Rally and demonstrate in every country and state. Let the United States Supreme Court and our government hear our voices: SILENCE NO MORE! WE WILL *NOT* GO BACK!

Thank you.

✺ Index ✺